Eaton Goodell Osman

Starved Rock

A Historical Sketch

Eaton Goodell Osman

Starved Rock
A Historical Sketch

ISBN/EAN: 9783743324879

Manufactured in Europe, USA, Canada, Australia, Japa

Cover: Foto ©ninafisch / pixelio.de

Manufactured and distributed by brebook publishing software (www.brebook.com)

Eaton Goodell Osman

Starved Rock

STARVED ROCK

A Historical Sketch

BY

EATON G. OSMAN

OTTAWA, ILL.
THE FREE TRADER PRINTING HOUSE
1895

COPYRIGHT BY
EATON G. OSMAN,
1895.

ENGRAVING BY
ILLINOIS ENGRAVING CO., CHICAGO.

PHOTOGRAPHS BY
GERDING, BOWMAN AND GUSTAVE KNEUSSL (AMATEUR),
OTTAWA, ILL.,
AND IRA B. MYERS (AMATEUR), CHICAGO.

DEER PARK, LOOKING DOWN THE GLEN.

PREFACE.

FRANCIS PARKMAN'S "La Salle and the Discovery of the Great West" must be hereafter the basis of any repetition of the story of the discovery and settlement of the Illinois river valley. That I have, in this little sketch, availed myself of the results of Dr. Parkman's labors will be apparent to every reader of his delightful volumes. I the more readily acknowledge this indebtedness in view of the fact that even before he had himself stood upon Starved Rock, his studies of the original authorities had led to his rejection of the supposition of Sparks and others, that it was Buffalo Rock which was the site of La Salle's famous "Rock Fort." Dr. Parkman established beyond question, from documents contemporary with La Salle, corroborating this conclusion of the student of manuscripts by subsequent personal observations on the ground, that Starved Rock was the true site of the ancient Fort St. Louis, around which was planted the first permanent settlement of the white race in the Mississippi valley, thus giving to Starved Rock a prestige historically equal to the fame it has ever had as a unique landmark of the Great West.

I have not attempted here to rewrite the history of the Illinois country, but simply to bring together in one place such authenticated facts relating to Starved Rock, scattered through many volumes, as may assist in giving the Rock its proper perspective on the canvas of western and our national history, as well as interest the thousands of strangers who annually visit this beautiful and interesting spot.

CONTENTS.

	PAGE
PREFACE,	3
INTRODUCTORY,	5
THE DISCOVERERS: Marquette and Joliet.	9
THE DISCOVERY: The Voyage of Marquette and Joliet,	12
THE FATE OF THE EXPLORERS: The Death of Marquette,	16
LA SALLE: His Dream of Empire.	19
LA SALLE'S CAREER: His Earlier Work,	22
TONTY: The Iroquois Raid,	25
STARVED ROCK FORTIFIED: La Salle Takes Possession.	28
KISMET: Failure and Death.	32
LA SALLE'S SUCCESSORS: Two Hundred Years Ago.	36
THE MISSIONS: The Immaculate Conception,	40
THE DRAMA OF THE EIGHTEENTH CENTURY: The Scenery of Tragedy,	44
STARVED ROCK IN THE EIGHTEENTH CENTURY: The Indian Sieges.	47
THE LAST OF THE ILLINI: The Final Tragedy,	53
THE SEQUEL: The Pottawatomies,	61
MODERN STARVED ROCK: The Era of the White Man,	65
THE HISTORIANS: Francis Parkman and John G. Shea,	69
THE NOVELIST: Mrs. Catherwood,	75
THE RELICS: Silent Witnesses,	77

VIEWS FROM TOP OF STARVED ROCK.

INTRODUCTORY.

> Here by this stream, in days of old
> The red men lived, who lie in mould;
> The leaves that once their history knew
> Their crumbling pages hide from view.

"I HAVE stood upon Starved Rock, and gazed for hours upon the beautiful landscape spread out before me," said the late Justice Sydney Breese.* "The undulating plains, rich in their verdure; the rounded hills beyond, clad in their forest livery; and the gentle river, pursuing its noiseless way to the Mississippi and the Gulf, all in harmonious association, make up a picture over which the eye delights to linger; and when to these are added the recollections of the heroic adventurers who first occupied it, that here the banner of France so many years floated freely in the winds; that here was civilization while all around was barbaric darkness,—the most intense and varied emotions cannot fail to be awakened."

Starved Rock is one of the most noted natural curiosities of the West. Once an arm of the bluff, which here bounds the Illinois river valley on the south, it now stands alone, an isolated sandstone cliff, whose walls, carved into form by the floods of countless generations, rise one hundred and twenty-five feet above the level of the river. Circular in form, the summit of the Rock contains about half an acre of land, which is well covered with a growth of evergreens and scrub-oaks, while its sides are draped with vines and ferns, wild flowers and cedars, and below

"The river calmly flows."

---
*BREESE: "*History of Illinois.*"

The summit is accessible only from the south, where the flood-eddies have heaped up the sands against the base. Nature's helping hand has been supplemented by man, both savage and civilized, who has carved rude steps in the rock, and converted a mere hint for a climbing pathway to the top into a practicable ascent.

Starved Rock stands apart, like a moss-grown and ivy-clad battle-tower of mediæval ages. It is a nature-made citadel, as impregnable to assault as Gibralter. Like many a feudal refuge, it has survived the attacks alike of war and time, and to-day stands a monument to brave men and their vanished dreams of political power and commercial aggrandizement.

From the summit, the valley of the Illinois for miles lies spread out before the eye as an open book—an incomparable view.

> "On either side the river lie
> Long fields of barley and of rye,
> That clothe the world and meet the sky;
> And through the fields the road runs by
> To many-towered Camelot

To the east the eye follows the thread of the river, as it flows past cultivated farms and under the shadow of verdure-clad hills. In the distance rises Buffalo Rock, a Starved Rock enlarged and magnified, behind which curls the smoke of Ottawa's busy shops; while afar in the haze beyond the hills of Rutland give shadowy form and contour to the vanishing horizon. On turning to the west, the eye lingers along the meandering stream on whose clear bosom once

> "Voyagers 'gainst time did row."

Stealing away through broad and fertile fields, or behind low clumps of trees, the silvery trail is at last lost in the far distance,

> "Where gleaming fields of haze
> Meet the voyageur's gaze."

In the midst of this haze may be distinguished the outlines of the twin cities of La Salle and Peru; while just below the horizon, extended from bluff to

bluff, the great bridge of the Illinois Central Railroad hangs suspended over the river,—
>Like a triumphal arch
>Erected o'er its march
>To the sea.

From the northern segment of the Rock, one looks down upon the river below his feet.
>"No wind stirs its waves,
>But the spirits of the braves
>Hov'ring o'er,
>Whose antiquated graves
>Its still water laves
>On the shore."

From the farther shore-line stretches the now cultivated meadow, where once stood the ancient Kaskaskia, the home of the savage tribes who two hundred years ago claimed and occupied the Illinois country as their hunting grounds. Under the brow of the distant bluff sits the village of Utica, wherein dwells but a tithe of the population that once lived upon this site.

It is and ever has been a rich and beautiful land, for whose possession many a desperate battle has been fought, both before and since the white man came; and the ashes of both the victor and the vanquished enrich the soil on which are grown the "corn and wine" of later generations of men who love the spot as dearly as did the fated red men. It is as beautiful now as then, but changed,—

>"Soft hints of meadows, sweet with hay;
>High banks that rise, thick fringed, between
>The wood and wave, forever green;
>A farm lawn, just beyond the way,
>Alive with youngsters at their play:
>All these in pictured landscape lie,
>Framed in pale hues of air and sky."

Deer Park—The Sentinel.

THE DISCOVERERS.

A fiery soul, which, working out its way,
Fretted the puny body to decay,
And o'er informed the tenement of clay.

Jacque marquette

MARQUETTE is one of the most interesting, as he is one of the most conspicuous, figures of Northwestern discovery. The scion of an illustrious family of French sheriffs and soldiers, whose later generations furnished three sons to die in the cause of American liberty as soldiers in the armies of our French allies in the War for Independence, Jacques, born at Laon in 1637, was destined to be the most celebrated of his race, as well as the last of that long line of priestly explorers and Christian martyrs whose names and deeds are the crown of glory of the Canadian church.

At the age of seventeen, Marquette entered the Society of Jesus and became a teacher. Later he chose a foreign missionary's career, and was sent to Canada (1666). At Three Rivers he devoted himself so assiduously to the study of Indian languages that he soon mastered six of the root tongues, with most of their dialects. It is probable that no man of his time had a more complete mastery of the Indian languages of the Northwest than Marquette. This learning soon came to be of immense value to him.

From Three Rivers he went (1668) to Sault de Ste. Marie, where with Dablon, his Father Superior, he built a church. In 1669 he went to Lapointe, at the western end of Lake Superior, where he met some of the

Illinois tribes, who had gone thither to trade, and who, he wrote, "are of apparently good disposition." They urged him to come among them, and he longed to do so; but Indian wars not only prevented his taking this step but moreover drove him back to the Straits; where he built a chapel, at St. Ignace, "the first sylvan shrine to Catholicity at Mackinaw."* To this laborious post the pious priest condemned himself, happy, though suffering all things, if as opportunity offered he might but have the blessed privilege of opening by the baptismal sacrament "the doors of bliss to the dying infant or more aged repenting sinner." Here he remained until summoned (1672) to join Joliet in the discovery and exploration of the Mississippi.

L. Jolliet

Joliet is one of "the lesser stars in the galaxy of American explorers and pioneers," a man who had no cotemporary biographer. Dr. John Gilmary Shea, by infinite labor, has been able to make but a bare outline sketch of his career, from which we obtain the following facts.

The son of a wagonmaker, Joliet was born in Canada in 1645. He was educated for the priesthood, but withdrew from the Society of Jesus to become a fur trader. He had, perhaps, says Dr. Shea, no distinct elements of character to raise him to greatness; but he appears to have been a man of considerable learning which he ultimately turned to good account. In his travels as a fur trader he obtained a thorough mastery of the Algonquin language and its dialects. Dablon says he was a man of the tact and prudence necessary to carry him through the Indian country; and furthermore he had "a courage to fear nothing where all is to be feared."

He had, prior to 1673, performed many perilous missions for his old friends, the Jesuits at Quebec, and had once been sent by the Colonial gov-

---

*SHEA: "*Discovery and Exploration of the Mississippi Valley.*"

ernment also to explore the copper mines of Lake Superior, of which Talon, the intendant, had heard many rumors. The immediate object of the journey failed of attainment, but the journey itself was one of great value in other respects. He had but returned from this adventure in the West when (1672) he was commissioned by Governor Frontenac to find and explore the Mississippi.

Starved Rock—The Pathway to the Top.

THE DISCOVERY.

> The wind blew fair; the white foam flew;
> The furrows followed free;
> We were the first that ever burst
> Into that silent sea.
> —*The Ancient Mariner*

THE VOYAGE OF MARQUETTE AND JOLIET.

JOLIET reached Point St. Ignace from Quebec on December 8, 1672, with his instructions from Governor Frontenac. Father Marquette's journal of this memorable voyage thus refers to Joliet's arrival:

"The day of the Immaculate Conception of the Holy Virgin, whom I had continually invoked since coming to the country of the Ottawas, to obtain from God the favor of being enabled to visit the nations on the river Mississippi - this very day was precisely that on which M. Joliet arrived with orders to go with him on this discovery. I was all the more delighted with this news because I saw my plans about to be accomplished, and found myself in the happy necessity of exposing my life for the salvation of all those tribes, especially the Illinois, who, when I was at St. Esprit, had begged me very earnestly to bring the word of God among them."

Champlain had founded Quebec in 1608, thus laying the corner stone of New France and "building the hive whence poured the swarm" of heroic Recollet and Jesuit Fathers, who within the next thirty-five years pushed their examination of the interior of the continent to the farthest limits of the St. Lawrence and the Great Lakes; and as the missions were pushed farther and farther westward, the annual *Relations* of the missionaries seldom failed to contain mention of the "great water" to the still farther west, of which

STARVED ROCK, LOOKING WEST FROM LOVER'S LEAP.

THE LIBRARY
OF THE
UNIVERSITY OF ILLINOIS

the good Fathers' Indian flocks gave them information. If, then, they had not themselves actually seen the river prior to 1673, the Fathers knew perfectly where it would be found and many details of the route to it; so that when Joliet and Marquette were commissioned by Talon to explore the river, they had only to follow a well known path to find it. Nevertheless, during the winter following Joliet's meeting with Marquette the two explorers made every preparation for their voyage, gathering information from the Indians concerning their route and the people they might encounter, determined, writes Marquette, that "if our enterprise was hazardous it should not be foolhardy."

On May 17, 1673, the explorers set out from St. Ignace, accompanied by five *voyageurs*, all in two birch-bark canoes. For the voyage they carried Indian corn and some jerked meat, as well as suitable goods as presents to the natives to be met on the way. "At the outset, Marquette placed the enterprise under the patronage of the Immaculate Virgin, promising that if she granted them success, the river should be named 'The Conception.' This pledge he strove to keep; but an Indian word, the very meaning of which has been disputed, is its designation."* Ascending the Fox river [of Wisconsin], crossing the portage to the Wisconsin and descending that river, on June 17th, they found themselves, probably first of white men [except Groseilliers and Radisson?] since DeSoto's companions fled from the midnight burial of their chief, on the bosom of the Father of Waters. We shall not follow them as they descended the mighty flood to a point below the mouth of the Arkansas. Having satisfied themselves that the river did not flow to the sea of Virginia, but to the Gulf of Mexico, they turned back, July 17, to the north "*

*HINSDALE: "*The Old Northwest.*" The Map is by Marquette (greatly reduced).

When they again reached the mouth of Illinois (Riviere de Divine)*, having been told by the Indians that here was the more direct route to the *Lac des Illinois*, they entered and followed it to the northeast, delighted with the stream and the country it watered. " We had never seen anything like this river," writes Marquette, " for the richness of the soil, the prairies and woods, the buffaloes, the elks, the deer, the wild cats, the bustards, the

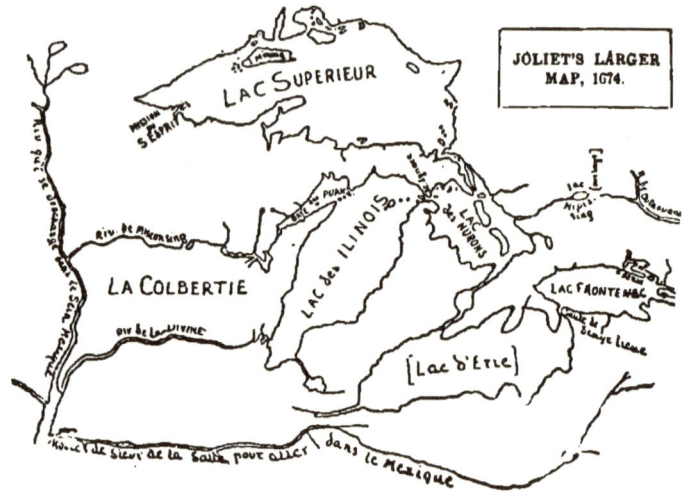

wild geese, the ducks, the paroquets and even the beavers. It is made up of little lakes and little rivers. That upon which we voyaged is wide, deep and gentle for sixty-five leagues."

In ascending the river Marquette records one stop, with the Peorias, an Illinois tribe, the location not being mentioned; but he says he here "baptized a dying infant a little while before it died, by an admirable providence,

---

* Joliet gave the Illinois the name Divine or Outrelaise, in compliment, it is supposed, to Frontenac's wife, noted for her beauty, and Mlle. Outrelaise, her facinating friend, who were called in court circles, *les divines.—Winsor.*

Joliet's Map is reduced from a reproduction in Winsor's "*Cartier to Frontenac.*"

for the salvation of its innocent soul," the tender record of undoubtedly the first baptism on Illinois river. Higher up the stream the voyagers found a village of the Illinois called Kaskaskia, containing seventy-four cabins, where, says Marquette, they were kindly received by the inhabitants, who, he adds, "compelled me to promise to return and instruct them."

This village was located on the north bank of the Illinois river, under the early morning shadow of Starved Rock; and Marquette's record is thus the first mention in history of "a place which has since become famous in the annals of western discovery."

The discoverers remained at Kaskaskia but a short time, and then one of the chiefs with his young men escorted them to the lake, *via* the Chicago portage, whence they returned at last to Green Bay, from which they had set out in the beginning of June.

"The great discovery by Joliet and Marquette did not at first prompt the French to any schemes for planting colonies to cultivate the rich lands of the Mississippi Valley, and a plan of settlement proposed by Joliet was rejected "* by the Court. It was only when the activity of the English in New York menaced the French fur trade that the struggle for dominion in the Mississippi Valley and the career of La Salle began.†

* SHEA: "*Catholic Church in Colonial Days.*"
† PARKMAN: "*La Salle and the Discovery of the Great West.*"

THE FATE OF THE EXPLORERS.

> Ah, weary priest! with pale hands
> On thy trobbing brow of pain.
> —*Whittier.*
>
> He was a man of comely form,
> Polished and brave, well learned and kind.
> —*Puritan Poet.*

THE DEATH OF MARQUETTE.

Wooden Anchor Used by the Early French Voyageurs.
Found in Green Bay.

MARQUETTE and Joliet separated at Green Bay, never again to meet. Marquette's constitution was so seriously impaired by the fatigues of the journey that he never afterward became a well man. Illness followed him so relentlessly that not until the following year was he able to complete his report and send it to his Father Superior at Quebec.

In the fall of the same year (1674) he received from Quebec an order to establish a mission at Kaskaskia, (Starved Rock) His heart was in the work; and on October 25 he left Green Bay for the Illinois His old malady, dysentery with hemorrhage, returning, however, he was compelled to winter with his white companions at the mouth of Chicago river, which place he left for the Illinois river, March 29, 1675, reaching Kaskaskia April 8 Here, on the plain north of and across the river from Starved Rock, he then founded the mission to which he gave his favorite name, "Immaculate Conception of the Blessed Virgin."

But it was only for a little while that he was able to teach the benighted Indians; for "continued illness soon obliged him to set forth on that return voyage which brought him to a lonely grave in the wilderness." On the eve of his departure from the village he convened the inhabitants to the number of two thousand, on a meadow hard by, and there, on a rude altar, exhibited four pictures of the Virgin Mary, explained their significance, and exhorted the chiefs and people to embrace Christianity.*

Quitting Kaskaskia soon after Easter, which occurred that year April 14, he returned to the Lake *via* the Kankakee portage and St. Joseph river. Unable to proceed further, his companions built for him a rude hut, near the mouth of the river, in which he died, with the names of Jesus and Mary on his lips and his face radiant with joy. He was buried on an eminence overlooking the lake, which he himself had pointed out for his resting place. But two years later his Indian friends from Mackinac removed his bones to St. Ignace, where they were buried in a vault under the floor of the log chapel. In process of time, the mission being afterwards abandoned, their resting place was forgotten ; but it was discovered in 1877 by a Michigan clergyman, and a monument has, by the latter's endeavors, been since erected to mark the spot.

Thus died, at the age of thirty-eight, one of the noblest and purest men whose names adorn the annals of the northwest.

JOLIET'S SUBSEQUENT CAREER.

M. Joliet reached Quebec in August, 1674, but within sight of Montreal was nearly drowned, losing all the records of his voyage. He made a verbal report to the Governor, accompanying it with a map made from recollection. He no doubt expected some substantial reward, but was disappointed, at least at that time, though for this and other services he was later granted the island of Anticosti at the mouth of the St. Lawrence, where in 1681 he established himself with his wife and six servants, and became interested in the fisheries. Being also a skilled navigator and surveyor, he was appointed by Frontenac hydrographer at Quebec. In 1690 the English commander, Sir William Phipps, burned Joliet's Anticosti establishment and took him and his wife prisoners. Joliet was subsequently released, and in 1694 explored Labrador on behalf of a seal and whale fishing company. He died,

*WALLACE : "*Illinois and Louisiana under French Rule.*"

evidently poor, in 1699 or 1700. His descendants appear to have inherited his virtues and his talent, and several of them have held positions of high trust and responsibility, both civil and ecclesiastical, in the modern Dominion of Canada.

FRONTENAC.
(Reproduced from a reduction, in Winsor's "Cartier to Frontenac," from Sulte's "Canadiens-Francais," Vol. ii.)

LA SALLE.

> I hear the tread of pioneers
> Of nations yet to be ;
> The first low wash of waves where soon
> Shall roll a human sea.
> — *Whittier.*

HIS DREAM OF EMPIRE.

IT HAS come to be the fashion in certain quarters to belittle the character and accomplishments of La Salle. While Parkman makes him second only to Champlain as the greatest of all French discoverers of the great west, Shea treats him as simply a follower of paths that others had previously blazed. Parkman bears testimony to the heroic persistence of the man in spite of immense physical difficulties and the more disheartening machinations of enemies, whose adverse influence was felt at every step of his career and at every point, from the court of Louis XIV. to the mouth of the Mississippi. Dr. Shea, on the other hand, ascribes his failure to a fatal lack of capacity as an explorer. "La Salle was doubtless a persuasive talker in setting forth his projects," he says, "though utterly incapable of carrying out even the simplest."

There is an element of truth in the latter view of La Salle, but the statement is an exaggeration of La Salle's real fault. It is true, La Salle, strictly speaking, discovered nothing except the Ohio river—neither the Mississippi nor its outlet, both of which had been seen by the Spaniard a hundred years before La Salle was born ; but these discoveries the Spaniard had also as long ago forgotten, and La Salle's claim of the land for France by right of discovery and occupancy was never disputed. As to the Northwest, though

La Salle was neither the first to explore its lakes or rivers, he certainly was the first to enter it as a settler and pioneer of the future settlers.

Moses* goss even further than Shea, attributing to La Salle a bickering spirit, which certainly is not a characteristic of the man as he is pictured by Parkman, confessedly the most competent historian of this period and department of our American history. Moses says:

"Had the French governor [Le Barre, La Salle's enemy at all times, as Frontenac was always his friend?] and La Salle pooled their issues, and instead of endeavoring to break each other down worked together, there was nothing to prevent their building up a colony at Fort St. Louis [Starved Rock] which would have been of great advantage to the interests of each, and exerted a controlling influence upon the destiny of New France. Had agriculture and permanent settlement been encouraged in connection with the traffic with the Indians, a prosperous and powerful community might have been established, which, growing and extending to other equally favorable localities in the Illinois country, might in fifty years have constituted a community which would have proved an insuperable barrier against any foreign encroachment, in consequence of its ability to maintain its own integrity. But the rapacity of one and the ambition of the other prevented the accomplishment of such a result."

Mr. Moses has overlooked the fact that this very idea was, in truth, the keynote of La Salle's career: that is, to take possession of and settle the Mississippi valley; but in this purpose he had the opposition of both Le Barre, the governor, and also the Jesuits, neither of whom then desired permanent settlers about them to interfere with their relations with the Indians. The responsibility of the failure of La Salle's attempts to colonize the Illinois rests much more with the court and the priesthood on the St. Lawrence than with La Salle on 'the Illinois. His failures, as the result of his own faults, must be attributed, not so much to the withering influences of a soul consumed with petty quarrels and bickerings, but rather to his unfortunate inability to create real friendships among his own people, and to his besetting

---

*JOHN MOSES: "*History of Illinois.*"

LOOKING NORTHWEST FROM TOP OF STARVED ROCK.

THE LIBRARY
OF THE
UNIVERSITY OF ILLINOIS

LA SALLE'S DREAM OF EMPIRE.

sin of trusting no one but himself, even in projects requiring for their success the co-operation of large bodies of men.*

More than two hundred years have passed since La Salle perished in the trackless wastes of the far Southwest, and his venturous soul fled to that "bourne from which no traveler returns"; but even as he stood upon the summit of Starved Rock in 1682 and 1683 and his eye swept over the magnificent landscape, his prophetic spirit saw in the then distant future the grandeur of the empire that was yet to come, whose very heart would throb in the fertile lands spread out before him, which he loved to characterize as "a terrestrial paradise." It was the master mind of La Salle that first conceived the policy which led on, step by step, from Starved Rock "to Fort Duquesne, Braddock's defeat, and Forbes's march to the Forks of the Ohio,' and the train of events culminating in the fall of Quebec. † Looking into the future, La Salle saw on these prairies and by the shores of the Great Lakes a New France far more powerful than the old, and this vision, one may truly say, was the guiding star of his romantic career. As the first white man to establish a settlement upon her soil, he has been justly styled

"the Father of Illinois"; but it was only when Wolfe triumphed on the Heights of Abraham that the empire which La Salle foresaw and devoted his life to found, became a historic fact. What La Salle did not see was that the great law of evolution had destined that this great power would be, not Norman but Anglo-Saxon. ‡

* PARKMAN: "*La Salle and the Discovery of the Great West.*"

† HINSDALE: "*The Old Northwest.*"

‡ JOHN FISKE: "*The Idea of God.*"

West End of Buffalo Rock.

LA SALLE'S CAREER.

Planting strange fruits and sunshine on the shore,
I make some coast alluring, some lone isle,
To distant men, who must go there or die.
—*Emerson.*

HIS EARLIER WORK.

ROBERT CAVALIER, Sieur de la Salle,—born in Rouen, 1643; educated for the priesthood; a Jesuit long enough to legally sacrifice his fortune because of the connection—came to America in 1666. With a small patrimony as capital he set up as a feudal lord at a place called La Chine, on lands granted him by the Seminary of St. Sulpice, at the most dangerous spot, perhaps, in North America.

It is clear that La Salle's purpose in coming to America was a greater one than to establish himself as landlord of a frightfully dangerous wilderness; for we find him studying Indian languages and Indian nature, both of which he came to understand thoroughly and completely. His relations with the natives were always singularly happy.

The establishment of La Salle at La Chine was a means only to a greater end. In 1669 he made his first expedition of discovery, and it is now generally conceded that in that year and in 1670 he explored the Ohio river at least to the falls at Louisville, and possibly to the Mississippi as well as the Illinois river.

In 1674, the discovery of Joliet and Marquette becoming known in Canada, disclosed the truth which La Salle had probably come to America to establish. If the latter were the fact, as seems probable, the current of his purpose was thereby changed. Since, therefore, the Spaniards had never taken possession of the Mississippi, it was La Salle's ambition now to profit by that oversight, and by reaching its mouth at the Gulf *via* the Illinois, he could take verbal possession, at least, of the valley, and by closing the mouth with a fort and by placing others along the rivers from the Lakes to the Gulf, he could hold it against all others, and thus add the best part of a continent to the possessions of Louis XIV. in America. Then the center of French dominion in North America could be transferred from bleak and inhospitable Canada to the fertile fields of the fruitful valley, which by agriculture and trade would sooner or later become a mighty empire. It was a grand and eminently practicable conception, which not many years after La Salle's death became the policy of the French government, with what success the history of the Franco-English struggle in America during the eighteenth cencentury amply testifies.

Returning to France in 1674, La Salle unfolded his great project at the court of Louis the Magnificent. In reward for his discovery of the Ohio he was ennobled; and having the friendship of Frontenac, the governor of Canada, he obtained liberal grants of lands and exclusive trading privileges both on Lake Ontario and in the new lands of the Illinois country, which he was to explore and settle—at his own individual expense, however.

In the summer of 1679, therefore, he built on Lake Erie the *Griffin*, the first vessel, except the Indian's canoe, to sail the great lakes; but while returning from Mackinac and Green Bay to Fort Frontenac with her first cargo of furs, the *Griffin* was lost with all on board.

La Salle meantime had pushed on to the St. Joseph river, at the mouth of which he built Fort Miamis, thus securing the key to the Illinois *via* the Kankakee. Here he heard rumors of the loss of the *Griffin*; but his purpose never faltered. Crossing the portage to the head waters of the Kankakee river, he launched eight canoes with thirty-five men, including the faithful

Tonty, upon the Illinois, down which he paddled until he came to Starved Rock, or, rather, to the great Indian town "La Vantum," on the plain north and west of the Rock. The town was deserted, but La Salle opened the corn *caches* of the Indians and removed such as he needed, leaving abundant presents in payment. Then he pushed on to the present Peoria lake, where he built another fort called Crevecœur, for he was now convinced, by the non-arrival of men and supplies of the *Griffin*, that his vessel was indeed lost.

Here he put another boat on the stocks, in which he purposed to sail to the mouth of the Mississippi; and then, leaving Tonty with fifteen of his men to complete the ship, he started for Canada to repair his loss. It was on this return journey, depressed by his loss and fearful for the future, that early in March, 1680, he a second time reached the Illinois town La Vantum, now buried in the desolation of very early spring. La Salle's men "saw buffalo wading in the snow, and they killed one of them."* On the following day, while the hunters were smoking the meat of the buffalo, La Salle went out to reconnoiter, and presently met three Indians, one of whom proved to be Chassagoac, the principal chief of the Illinois. The interview (with the latter) was so favorable that the chief at its close promised to befriend Tonty at Crevecœur. "After several days spent at the deserted town, La Salle prepared to resume his journey," says Parkman. "Before his departure his attention was attracted to the remarkable cliff of yellow sandstone, now called Starved Rock, a mile or more above the village,—a natural fortress, which a score of resolute white men might make good against a host of savages; and [when he arrived at Fort Miamis and found two of his men there waiting for him, he sent by them to] Tonty an order to examine it and make it his stronghold in case of need."† The Rock was indeed admirably adapted for La Salle's purpose. It commanded the river, the highway for all travel from the Lakes to the Gulf, and in addition to being in the midst of a fertile country, it overlooked the great town which would be the center of an immense Indian traffic.

---
*PARKMAN: "*La Salle*," etc., p. 177.
†PARKMAN: "*La Salle*," etc., p. 178.

Hear ye not the shrill piping screams on the air?
Up, Braves! For the conflict prepare ye—prepare!
Aroused from the canebrake, far south, by your drum,
With beaks whet for carnage, the Battle Birds come.
    *   *   *   *   *   *
On the forehead of Earth strikes the Sun in his might,
Oh, gibe me with glances as searching as light,
In the front of the onslaught to single each crest,
Till my hatchet grows red on their bravest and best.*
                                          —*Indian War Song.*

THE IROQUOIS RAID.

LA SALLE had scarcely bade farewell to Tonty at Crevecœur when eight of the men with the latter, discouraged by the news brought by La Salle's messengers to Tonty from Fort Miamis, of the loss of the *Griffin*, mutinied, and having plundered the fort and destroyed the ship, deserted while Tonty was examining Starved Rock in accordance with La Salle's order. Having sent four men by different routes to Canada to inform La Salle of this latest disaster, Tonty was left at the Rock with but five white companions, two of whom were Membre and Ribourde, Recollet friars.

For greater show of confidence, this little band of La Salle's faithful

---

*WAR SONG—Pe-na-se-wug. From the Algonquin of Schoolcraft, by C. F. Hoffman. See Schoolcraft's "*Western Scenes.*"

followers took up their residence with the Indians, hoping to maintain themselves until La Salle's return. Here they spent the opening spring and summer. The Illinois among whom they dwelt were an aggregation of distinct though kindred tribes--the Kaskaskias, the Peorias, the Kahokias, the Tamaroas, the 'Moingona and others,* and were reputed a cowardly and rather contemptible race of Indians.

The summer had passed uneventfully, and "for the Frenchmen time doubtless hung heavy on their hands; for nothing can surpass the vacant monotony of an Indian town when there is neither hunting, nor war, nor feasts, nor dancing, nor gambling to beguile the lagging hours." And so out of the interminable monotony came the 10th of September; when "suddenly the village was awakened from its lethargy as by the crash of a thunderbolt." An army of Iroquois from New York had been seen approaching to attack them. On the 11th the attack came. Tonty and his few men, who then were suspected as allies of the Iroquois and had the day before barely escaped with their lives from the infuriated Illinois, joined with the latter, who were greatly outnumbered by the Iroquois.

The scene of the struggle was the prairie just at the edge of the woods bordering the Big Vermilion river near its mouth. The Illinois had crossed the river now bearing their name and had attacked the enemy, when Tonty, desirous at all hazards, for the sake of La Salle's interests, of preserving peace, or at least of saving the Illinois from their almost certain massacre, attempted to mediate, and, at infinite personal risk, did obtain a cessation of the battle and a promise from the Iroquois, who were at peace, nominally at least, with the French, to abandon their purpose.

The Iroquois, however, soon repented and as quickly violated all their promises. Tonty and his followers were compelled to leave the village and that part of the country, while the Iroquois, balked of their living prey, "wreaked their fury on the Illinois dead. They dug up the graves, they threw down the scaffolds. Some of the bodies they burned ; some they threw

*PARKMAN : " *La Salle*," etc., 207 *et seq.*

to the dogs; some, it is affirmed, they ate."* The Illinois had escaped down the river by keeping together as a compact mass until they reached its mouth. Then some crossed the Mississippi to the western side; others continued on down the river, while the Tamaroas, remaining near the mouth of the Illinois, were destroyed by the Iroquois.

La Salle with four men reached the scene on his return from Canada in November. But no saluting whoop greeted their ears from the village, as they had expected. "They passed Starved Rock, but as La Salle ascended its lofty top he saw no palisades, no cabins, no sign of human hand, and still its primeval crest of forest overhung the gliding river."† The town was desolate. They landed. "Before them lay a plain once swarming with wild human life, now a waste of devastation and death. * * Near at hand was the burial ground of the village. The travelers sickened with horror as they entered its revolting precincts. * * Every grave had been rifled. A hyena warfare had been waged against the dead. La Salle knew the work of the Iroquois."

La Salle was consumed with alarm for the fate of Tonty; but finding no trace of white men among the remains, he hoped to find him still alive, and in that hope pushed on to the mouth of the Illinois, trusting to get some clue to his fate or his whereabouts. At the mouth of the river he abandoned the trail and returned to Fort Miamis, where he spent the winter, while Tonty and his companions, after most fearful suffering, found a refuge at Green Bay.

---
*PARKMAN: *Ibid.*, p. 218. This Indian battle is described by Parkman in a most spirited chapter, to which the reader is referred.
†PARKMAN: *Ibid.* p. 191 *et seq.*

STARVED ROCK FORTIFIED.

> Strangers came to build a tower,
> And threw their ashes overland.
> —*Thoreau.*

LA SALLE TAKES POSSESSION.

LA SALLE spent the winter of 1680-81 at Fort Miamis, organizing a league of the western Indians to resist the Iroquois, the league's principal town to be located near the Rock on Illinois river. Then he returned to Canada *via* Mackinac, where he again met Tonty. Having arranged his affairs, he returned in November, 1681, to Fort Miamis, where he found his Indian allies, with eighteen of whom and twenty-three Frenchmen, including Tonty, he set out again for the Illinois. They passed the site of the future Chicago, January 4, 1862, and pushed on without stopping to the mouth of the Mississippi, which he reached April 9, 1682. Here La Salle, "in the name of the most high, mighty, invincible Prince, Louis fourteenth of the name," took possession of the country and named it Louisiana, "the weather-beaten voyagers joining their voices in the great hymn of *Vexilla Regis*, which closed the ceremony"—

> "The Banners of Heaven's King advance,
> The mystery of the Cross shines forth."

"On that day the realm of France received on parchment a stupendous accession"—a region that stretched from the Alleghenies to the Rocky Mountains, from the Rio Grande and the Gulf to the farthest springs of the Missouri,—"all by the virtue of a feeble human voice, inaudible at half a mile."*

---
*PARKMAN: "*La Salle*," etc.

LA SALLE.

NOTE.—The above portrait is said by Winsor, in "Narrative and Critical History," to be based on an engraving preserved in the library of Rouen, entitled "Cavilli de la Salle François," and is the only picture of La Salle, except one, meriting notice.

THE LIBRARY
OF THE
UNIVERSITY OF ILLINOIS

La Salle had now written his name in history; there remained the greater task of consummating the schemes of his pregnant brain: the founding of a permanent colony on the Illinois and the abandonment of the route to France *via* Canada for one *via* Mississippi and the Gulf. The Illinois colony at Starved Rock, the key of the situation, was to serve "the double purpose of a bulwark against the Iroquois and a place of storage for the furs of all the western tribes; and he hoped in the following year to secure an outlet for this colony and for all the trade of the valley of the Mississippi by occupying the mouth of that river by a fort and another colony."*

At the moment of his triumph, as he returned from the Gulf, La Salle was taken with a dangerous illness and became unable to proceed. He sent Tonty forward to Mackinac, therefore, to dispatch his report to France and then repair to the Rock. In September, however, the two men met at Mackinac, where, hearing a rumor of a coming attack on the western Indians by the Iroquois (which if successful would be the ruination of his project), La Salle abandoned his intention of going immediately to France, and with Tonty, repaired at once to the Rock, where, in December, 1682, they began to entrench themselves. "They cut away the forest that crowned the Rock, built storehouses and dwellings of its remains, dragged timber up the rugged pathway, and encircled the summit with a palisade."

Thus the winter passed. The Indians, who saw in La Salle their defense from the Iroquois, "gathered around his stronghold like the timerous peasantry of the middle ages round the rock built castle of their feudal lord. From the wooden ramparts of St. Louis, high and inaccessible as an eagle's nest, . . . La Salle looked down on a concourse of wild human life. Lodges of bark and rushes, or cabins of logs, were clustered on the open plain or along the edges of the bordering forests Squaws labored, warriors lounged in the sun, naked children whooped and gamboled on the grass Beyond the river, a mile and a half to the left, the banks were studded once more with the lodges of the Illinois, who to the number of six thousand had returned since their defeat to this their favorite dwelling place. Scattered

*PARKMAN: "*La Salle*," etc,

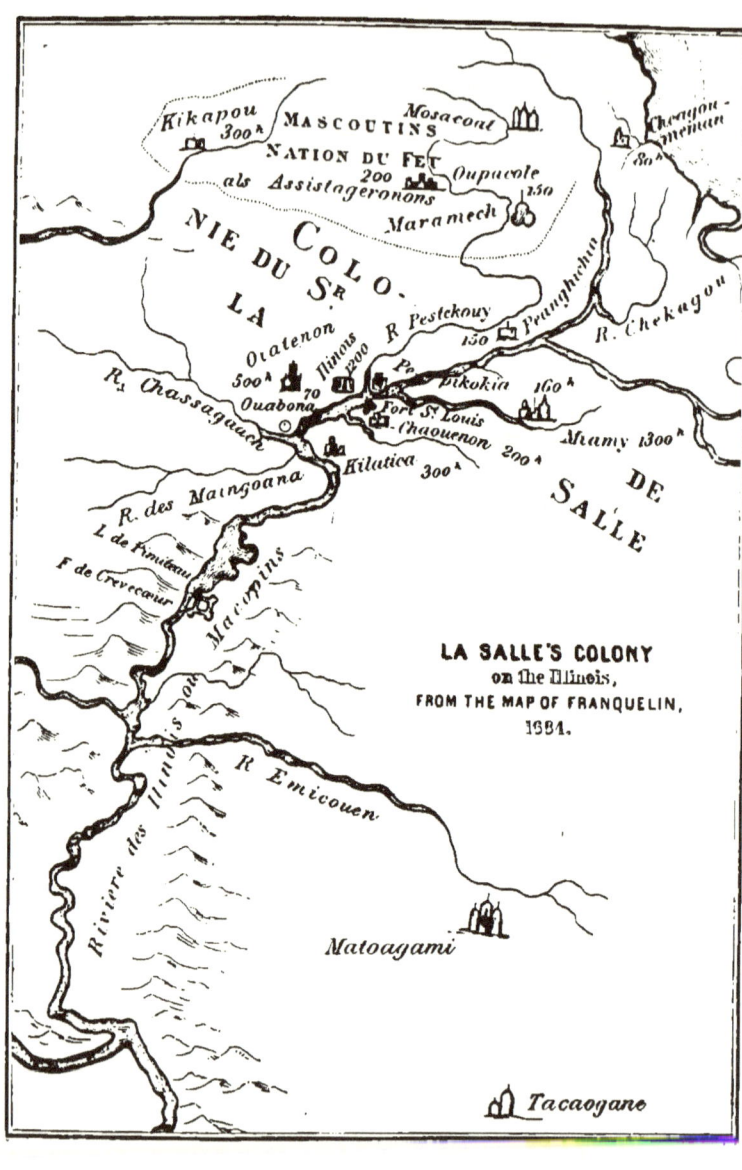

along the valley, or over the neighboring prairie, were the cantonments of a half score of other tribes, and fragments of tribes, gathered under the protecting ægis of the French—Shawanoes from the Ohio, Abenakis from Maine, Miamis from the sources of the Kankakee, with others whose barbarous names are hardly worth the record [in all four thousand warriors, or twenty thousand souls]. Nor were these La Salle's only dependents. By the terms of his patent he held seignorial rights over this wild domain; and he now began to grant it out in parcels to his followers. These, however, were as yet but a score; a lawless band, trained in forest license." *

The village of the Shawanoes was probably located on the edge of the bluff south of Starved Rock, at the intersection of the two ravines, where the remains of their rude earthwork may still be traced.

*PARKMAN : "*La Salle,*" etc., p. 295 *et seq.* The Map, p. 30, is from the same work. The picture below is from " *Wisconsin,*" in " The Stories of the States " series of histories.

Taking Possession of Louisiana.

KISMET.

> The sequel of to-day unsolders all
> The goodliest fellowship of famous Knights
> Whereof this world has record. Such a sleep
> They sleep—the men I loved.
> — *Tennyson:* " *Morte d'Arthur.*"

FAILURE AND DEATH.

IN spite of difficulties and hindrances which to other men would have seemed insurmountable, La Salle had succeeded, and the corner stone of a new empire had been laid. It only remained to rear the superstructure on La Salle's foundation. Unfortunately, Frontenac had been recalled and Le Barre in Canada "reigned in his stead." La Salle had his faults; but withal, had Le Barre been his friend, as he might have been, and not his enemy, as he was, the course of American history might have been changed.

La Salle plead with Le Barre for his rights and to be freed from the machinations of courtiers, fur traders and an unfriendly priesthood, but all in vain. The colony in its present state was, therefore, foreordained to failure. Whereupon La Salle, leaving the faithful Tonty to protect his interests on the Illinois, proceeded to France to organize a colony which should proceed to the Illinois *via* the Gulf and the Mississippi, taking possession of the mouth of the latter; and thus La Salle and the Illinois could be freed from their perennial menace, the provincial government at Quebec

As always at the court of Louis, La Salle was successful. Several vessels and some four hundred colonists sailed in 1684 for the Mississippi, while La Forest was specially commissioned to take command of La Salle's property in Canada, and Tonty restored to the command at Fort St. Louis,

Le Barre being in a letter accompaning these commissions especially scourged by his royal master, the King.

Unfortunately, the command of the vessels while at sea was given to another; there was friction among the leaders, and finally a storm drove them to a haven west of the mouth of the great river, and a landing was effected on the shore of the present state of Texas. The rest is a tale of miserable disappointment, suffering, treachery, failure and death. While making a journey in search of the lost Mississippi La Salle was murdered by his own men on Trinity river, Texas, March 19, 1687. A few of the colonists, including his brother, Jean Cavelier, and the faithful Joutel, reached Fort St. Louis (Starved Rock); a few had returned to France; the rest misserably perished.

"Thus in the vigor of his manhood, at the age of forty-three, died Robert Cavelier de la Salle, 'one of the greatest men,' writes Tonty, 'of the age'; without question one of the most remarkable explorers whose names live in history."

"It is easy to reckon up his defects, but it is not easy to hide from sight the Roman virtues that redeemed them," writes Parkman. "Beset by a throng of enemies, he stands, like the King of Isarel, head and shoulders above them all. He was a tower of adamant, against whose impregnable front hardship and danger, the rage of man and of the elements, the southern sun, the northern blast, fatigue, famine and disease, delay, disappointment and deferred hope emptied their quivers in vain. That very pride, which Coriolanus like, declared itself most sternly in the thickest

Rock Climbers.

The Murther of Monsr. de La Salle

NOTE.—This is a reproduction (from Windsor: "Narrative and Critical History of America") of a reproduction in Margry's "Memories," etc., of an old copper plate published a few years after La Salle's death. It was by Van der Gucht, and appears in the London edition (1698) of Hennepin's "New Discovery." The face of La Salle, enlarged, appears as the initial to a previous chapter of this "Sketch" (p. 22.)

press of foes, has in it something to challenge admiration. Never, under the impenetrable mail of paladin or crusader, beat a heart of more intrepid metal than within the stoic panoply that armed the breast of La Salle. To estimate aright the marvels of his patient fortitude one must follow his track through the vast scene of his interminable journeyings, those thousands of weary miles of forest, marsh and river, where again and again, in the bitterness of baffled striving, the untiring pilgrim pushed onward toward the goal which he never was to attain. America owes him an enduring memory; for, in this masculine figure, she sees the pioneer who guided her to the possession of her richest heritage."

The Lambert Tree Statue of La Salle,
Lincoln Park, Chicago.

LA SALLE'S SUCCESSORS.

His step is firm, his eye is keen,
Nor years in brawl and battle spent,
Nor toil, nor wounds, nor pain have bent
The lordly frame of old Castin.
— *Scott.*

TWO HUNDRED YEARS AGO.

Henry de Tonty

A veteran of the Sicilian wars, in which he had a hand blown off by a grenade, whom La Salle met in Paris in 1678, is one of the most superb figures in the annals of the Mississippi valley. His industry and energy, his bravery and his tact, his integrity and his faithfulness, his honorable character and amiable disposition, unite to differentiate him from all those whose names as the lesser stars crowd the earlier pages of those annals. Parkman calls him, "That brave, loyal and generous man, always vigilant and always active, beloved and feared alike by white man and by red." Mrs. Catherwood* says: "La Salle is a definite figure in the popular mind. But La Salle's greater friend is known only to historians and students. To me the finest fact in the Norman explorer's career is the devotion he commanded in Henri de Tonty. No stupid dreamer, no ruffian at heart, no betrayer of friendships, no mere blundering woodsman—as La Salle has been outlined by his enemies—could have bound to himself such a man as Tonty.

*Mrs. Mary Hartwell Catherwood; "*The Story of Tonty.*"

STARVED ROCK, FROM SOUTHEAST.

THE LIBRARY
OF THE
UNIVERSITY OF ILLINOIS

The love of this friend, and the words this friend has left on record, thus honor La Salle. And we who like courage and steadfastness and gentle courtesy in man owe much honor which has never been paid to Henri de Tonty."

Tonty, while La Salle was making his last voyage to France, was removed from the command of Fort St Louis by order of Le Barre, who was determined to ruin La Salle; but he remained to keep watch and ward over La Salle's interests at La Rocher. The next year, however, the King reinstated him as La Salle's commandant at the Rock. He no sooner heard at Mackinac of La Salle's landing and earlier disasters on the Gulf, than he prepared at his own cost an expedition for his relief, composed of twenty-five Frenchmen and eleven Indians. He went to the mouth of the Mississippi, but finding no trace of the colony, returned to the Arkansas, where six of his men volunteered to remain, two of whom afterwards rescued La Salle's brother, Cavelier, Joutel and others, who, with unpardonable ingratitude, carefully concealed the fact of La Salle's death, even while they accepted for months Tonty's hospitality on Starved Rock, and took from him, on La Salle's contingent order written before his death, furs sufficient to carry Cavelier, at least, in good circumstances back to France.

Tonty after La Salle's death, remained some time in command of Fort St. Louis as La Salle's representative. In 1690, however, he addressed a petition to Ponchartrain, the minister at Paris, reciting that though he was commissioned and had served as captain for many years, he had received no pay. Frontenac, who by this time was again Governor of Canada, endorsed Tonty's petition, in consequence of which he and La Forest, another faithful lieutenant of La Salle, were granted the proprietorship of Fort St. Louis, where they carried on a trade in furs.

The station was a most important one, as we have seen, both politically and commercially. It was the most considerable Indian village in the Illinois country, having a population ranging, according to circumstances, from nothing to twenty thousand souls, but averaging, at times of peace, about eight thousand. The lodges were built along the river bank for a distance of a mile or more, while the meadows were extensively cultivated, yielding large crops, chiefly of Indian corn.

In 1696, the King issued an order "abandoning Mackillimackinac and other outposts on the lakes, as well as all other advanced posts except Fort St. Louis, in the Illinois, which the King wishes maintained on condition that Sieurs De la Forest and Tonti, to whom he reserves the concession, should not bring or cause to be brought any beaver into the colony." Charlevoix* says: " I have been unable to ascertain on whose advice the King's council adopted this resolution. The excursions of the Canadians into new countries certainly ruined the commerce of New France [Canada]; introduced frightful libertinage; rendered the nation contemptible among all the tribes on the continent, and raised insurmountable obstacles to the progress of religion."

Whatever the cause of the above order, it is true that during the few years after La Salle's death the influence and trade of the Rock declined, both because of the dispersion of the resident tribes by Indian raids, and also because the influences at work in Canada against La Salle and his project had succeeded in changing the route to the Mississippi from the Illinois to that *via* the Fox river portage to the Wisconsin †

In 1702 Tonty was directed to join D'Iberville in lower Louisiana, while La Forest was recalled to Canada. Then for the first time the fort was officially abandoned. It was re-occupied from time to time by *coureurs des bois*, as an illicit trading post, and formally again in 1718, when a number

---

*CHARLEVOIX: "*History of New France*," V., 131.
†WALLACE: "*Illinois and Louisiana under French Rule.*"

Canyon near Starved Rock.

of traders resided there; but when Charlevoix passed down the river in 1721 he found it abandoned, only the ruins of its palisades remaining.*

But little is known of Tonty after he joined D'Iberville; and Charlevoix says he died at Fort St. Louis on the Mobile river, at about the age of fifty-four. N. Matson,† of Princeton, in his lifetime a collector of Indian and French Indian reminiscences, has printed a tradition, which he says he heard from descendants of the old coureurs, old residents now on the American Bottom, who had it as it was handed down from father to son, as was the custom among primitive peoples everywhere. The story is that Tonty, years after 1702, returned to the Rock, an old and broken man, where he died, revealing his identity at the supreme moment to the awe-struck Indians and traders who had borne him to the summit where he had so long commanded. Let us hope, if Tonty's brave heart and gentle spirit could find solace and rest dying here, that it was so. But if, as this legend further says, Tonty's body was buried at the foot of Starved Rock where the waters of the quiet Illinois would wash its southern segment, the living of to-day have still a duty to perform: the erection of a stone to mark his last resting place.

*PARKMAN : "La Salle, etc.," 411. Note.
†MATSON : "French and Indians on Illinois River."

THE MISSIONS.

> Oh, the generations old,
> Over whom no church-bells tolled,
> Christless, lifting up blind eyes
> To the silence of the skies.
>
> The bells of the Roman mission
> That call from their turrets twain
> To the boatman on the river,
> To the hunter on the plain.
> —*Whittier*.

THE IMMACULATE CONCEPTION.

THE earlier American Catholic missionaries to the Indians of North America were to a degree distinguished for "heroic self-devotion, energy of purpose, purity of motive, holiness of design." Nowhere can be found "more that is sublime even to eyes blinded by the glare of human greatness" than in the biographies of these martyrs of the American wilderness. Parkman's volume, "The Jesuits in North America," is one continuous tale of Christian heroism and zeal, which has not been surpassed by any age of the church in any clime. The missionaries who sacrificed all things, suffered all things, endured all things, had not all passed from earth until these men, at least, had met death for Christ's sake and his church.

We have seen how, in 1675, the gentle Marquette, the last of this line of Jesuit martyrs, established at the Illinois town the mission which he called the "Immaculate Conception"; how, reaching the village, April 8, he went from cabin to cabin instructing the inmates. "Then, when all were sufficiently aware of the doctrines of the Cross to follow his discourse, he convoked a general meeting on a beautiful prairie. There before their wondering eyes he raised his altar, and .'. they beheld him offer the holy sacrifice of the mass, on the very day when, over sixteen centuries before, the God he preached had instituted it in the upper room in Jerusalem. Thus on Maundy Thursday was possession taken of Illinois in the name of Catholicity —of Jesus and of Mary."*

Claude Allouez. Two years later the indefatigable Claude Allouez was sent to Kaskaskia, as this great town was known to the churchmen. He arrived April 27, 1676, and was immediately lodged in Marquette's cabin. He worked hard, and on May 3, the feast of the Invention of the Holy Cross, he erected in the midst of the village a cross twenty-five feet high ; but though he baptised thirty-five infants and one adult, his mission at that time has not been counted a success. He was again at Kaskaskia in 1678, remaining until 1679, when he retired before the approach of La Salle.

Though La Salle had an aversion to the Jesuits in general, who, he always believed, and with some reason, were his enemies, and a dislike to Allouez in particular, he was still a profoundly religious man, and was invariably accompanied in his expeditions by the "Black Gowns," notably the Recollet fathers Gabriel de la Ribourde, Zenobius Membre and Louis Hennepin In the year 1680 the two former took up the work abandoned by Allouez, and were with Tonty on the memorable day described on pages 26 and 27. After their escape from the Iroquois, Tonty and his Frenchmen and the two Fathers embarked, September 18, for Green Bay. On the next day, when the men were repairing their injured canoe, the aged Father Ribourde retired apart to say his breviary. While thus engaged, he was met by a party of Kickapoos, out against the Iroquois, who ruthlessly murdered him.† Thus, in his seventieth year, and in the fortieth of his priesthood, perished this last scion of a noble Burgundian house, who had renounced the world and its honors and the comforts of Europe for the wilds of Canada and a martyr's death.

*SHEA: *"Catholic Missions among the Indian Tribes of the United States."*
†SHEA: *Ibid.*

In 1680 Allouez returned to the mission, remaining there until Cavelier, Joutel, Father Douay and the other survivors of La Salle's ill-fated colony arrived from Texas. As these men falsely said that La Salle was still alive and on his way to the Rock, Allouez again retired. Little is known of him after this time, except that he died at La Salle's Fort Miamis in 1690, leaving a name imperishably connected with the discovery of the Great West.

The year Allouez left Kaskaskia, Father James Gravier visited Illinois, but at that time his mission did not become a permanent one; and the real successor of Allouez was the famous Sebastian Rale, who was sent thither from Quebec, arriving in the spring of 1682. He found a town of three hundred cabins, of four to five fires each, two families to a fire; and a banquet in his honor was given by the head chief. Yet, though he was heartily welcomed, the faith he preached made but slow progress. After a two years' stay with the Illinois, Father Rale was recalled to his original charge, the Abenakis on the Kennebec river in Maine *

Father Gravier came a second time to the Kaskaskia mission in March, 1694, and built a chapel within the fort on Starved Rock, by Tonty's permission. He also built a second chapel outside the fort among the Indians, and "planted before it a towering cross amid the shouts and musketry of the French." He remained in general charge of the mission until 1697, when he was recalled to Mackinac. He was succeeded by Fathers Julius Binneteau and James Pinet.

Widow's Run Canyon.

*His career there is intensely interesting; and will be found in detail in Francis Parkman's "*A Half Century of Conflict*," Vol. 1.

Father Gravier's mission seems to have been the most successful of all, in which work he was not a little assisted by Mary, daughter of the chief and wife of Michael Ako (or d'Acau.) Ako was probably one of Hennepin's companions in his voyage up the Mississippi, who on his return to the Illinois wished to marry the Indian maiden against her will but with the consent of her father. Father Gravier sided with the maiden, who at length yielded to her parent's wish in the hope that she might, by this self-sacrifice, be the means of bringing both Ako and her parents into the fold of Christ. Ultimately her wish we are told by Dr. Shea, in a sympathetic chapter, was fully gratified, she having been the means of bringing many souls to the church. Father Gravier was the first to analyze the Illinois language and compile its grammar and its dictionary, but none of his works are said now to exist except in bare fragments.

In 1698 came Father Marest, under whose guidance and direction the mission was removed to the new Kaskaskia (the Kaskaskia of our time—the first capital of the state of Illinois), on the banks of the Mississippi. This migration of missionaries and Indians, which took place in the year 1699, was the natural result of the decay of the Rock's importance as a military and commercial point, and of a desire for consolidation by the western, or Illinois, tribes against the Iroquois and those firebrands of the west, the Foxes.

[NOTE.—Those who are interested in the annals of the missions may consult Wallace and Shea, *supra;* also John Kip's "*Jesuit Missions*" and "*Illinois in the Eighteenth Century*" (Fergus Historical Series), by Hon. E. G. Mason.]

THE DRAMA OF THE EIGHTEENTH CENTURY.

> God said, I am tired of kings,
> I suffer them no more;
>   *   *   *   *
> My angel,—his name is Freedom,—
> Choose him to be your King;
> He shall cut pathways east and west,
> And fend you with his wing.
> —*Emerson.*

THE SCENERY OF TRAGEDY.

STARVED ROCK played its humble role —or, rather, was a part of the *mise en scene* of the momentous drama of the eighteenth century, when the great struggle took place between freedom and absolutism for the possession of the fairest and greatest part of the North American continent When the century opened, the French empire in America was at the flood tide of its prosperity. The triple alliance of priest, soldier and trader had with unerring instinct and judgment taken possession of every route to the interior of the continent, and had so united the native tribes in the French interest that Canada and her western frontier were deemed so secure that, as we have seen, most of the distant garrisons were withdrawn as unnecessary to the preservation of colonial autonomy. In the far South, though La Salle's schemes had come to naught, they had been revived seven years after his death by Tonty, who had successfully "urged the seizure of Louisiana for three reasons: firstly, as a base of attack upon Mexico; secondly, as a depot for the furs and lead ores of the interior; and thirdly, as the only means of preventing the English from becoming masters of the west."*

---

*PARKMAN: "*A Half Century of Conflict.*"

LOOKING SOUTHEAST FROM STARVED ROCK.

THE LIBRARY
OF THE
UNIVERSITY OF ILLINOIS

More successful than La Salle, D'Iberville, though he built his fort at Biloxi [state of Mississippi] and not on the river, had actually taken possession of the mouth of the Mississippi, thus outwitting the English, who were in fact on the point of seizing the river, and retarding for more than a hundred years the development of Louisiana on lines of English freedom. New France had, therefore, two heads: one looking to the Gulf of St. Lawrence, the other to the Gulf of Mexico; and if the northern wing of the empire had its hardly concealed jealousy of the southern end, it nevertheless appreciated the value of the latter as an aid to stem the incoming tide of English influence in the north.

One strategic mistake only had the builders of the Franco-American empire made, but it was vital—irremediable: they had neglected the Mohawk and Hudson rivers of New York, which were occupied by the Dutch, who were even shrewder traders than the French and more far-seeing Up to about this time, too, the English had been content to occupy as agriculturists a narrow strip along the Atlantic coast, where they busied themselves, and, fortunately for future generations, worried themselves, too, and their governors, with questions of political and religious rights and privileges, rather than with what the continent contained behind the Appalachian wall which few of them cared to penetrate or to cross. The Hudson and the Mohawk rivers however pierced that wall; and when now the Dutch possessions in New York came into the hands of the English, the character of the Albany colony did not wholly change, but the Englishman began to appreciate the possibilities of the vast interior for trade; for he even then was a more successful trader than even the Dutchman.

For twenty five years the English traders had been established on Hudson's Bay, diverting the northern trade of New France from the St. Lawrence. If now the English should also get a foot-hold on the Great Lakes and in the famous beaver country of the present Michigan peninsula, the northern wing of New France would be hemmed within very narrow limits indeed, and her trade ruined by the cheaper and better goods of the Yankees.

The cession to the English by the Iroquois in 1701 of all their claims to the country formerly occupied by the Hurons precipitated the struggle which the shrewd Count Frontenac had long foreseen, but which the politico-clerical influence with his successors and the proverbial corruption of the court at Quebec had left the colony more or less unprepared to meet. These Iroquois lands were bounded by the Lakes Ontario, Huron and Erie, "containing in length about 800 miles and in breadth 400 miles, including the country where beavers and all sorts of wild game keep."* They pierced the very heart of New France.

The problem, then, that confronted the French authorities at Quebec was how to stem this unpropitious tide. The building of a Fort at Detroit by La Mothe Cadillac was the first step in opposition. Another step in the same direction brings us back again to Starved Rock and the Illinois.

* HINSDALE: " *The Old Northwest.*"

STARVED ROCK IN THE EIGHTEENTH CENTURY.

> Freedom all winged expands,
> Nor perches in a narrow place;
> Her broad van seeks unplanted lands.
> —*Emerson.*

THE INDIAN SIEGES.

WHEREVER the French came in contact with them, their relations to the Indians were for the most part singularly felicitous. This fact may find explanation, aside from the natural adaptability of the French, in the circumstance that they made no effort to dispossess the Indians of their lands or hunting grounds. It was, at least tacitly, agreed that the savages should be left in undisturbed possession of the whole of the vast domain of the West on condition that they allowed the French to control or monopolize its trade.* Besides, the *coureurs des bois*, who made New France and built the chain of forts which bound the West to Canada, though proud of their French blood and language, were in the bush quite as much Indian as French, and thus they had immense influence over them. Above all, the *coureurs* hated the English; and being the shrewdest of diplomats they won over the Indians to themselves, and both patrolled the forests and lakes as against the venturesome Englishmen. Even the Iroquois had become neutral for the time, and the destiny of America seemed already decided; for " the lilies of France floated without opposition over the entire expanse from Quebec to the mouth of the Mississippi, and from the Alleghenies to the base of the Rocky Mountains."†

---
*HEBBERD: " *Wisconsin under the Dominion of France.*"
†HEBBERD: *Ibid.*

But the curse of Canada was the monopoly held by the one trading company which had legal control of all the commerce of the colony, and whose goods were not only poorer but were extortionately high as compared with those of the English. The Indians were not slow to discover this difference, and they began to chafe under the French trading yoke. This was especially true of the Foxes of Wisconsin, a nation whose renown for bravery, independence, intractability and endurance was then second to that of no tribe of the West. The behavior of the Foxes so exasperated the French authorities that it was understood (at least among the Indian allies of the French) that the governor desired the utter extermination of the Fox nation.* The massacre of a large part of them at Detroit in 1712 may or may not have been deliberately planned by the French; but it seems to have been so understood by the allies, who, after the siege was over wherein several hundred Foxes were butchered, set out for Quebec to claim the reward which they insisted the governor had promised for the Foxes' destruction.†

The tragedy at Detroit,‡ though it crippled the Fox nation, did not destroy it, nor break the spirit of these indomitable savages; it only deepened their dislike of the French into a grim and undying hatred. After a short truce, during which they made an alliance with the Sioux, the Foxes, in small war parties, began to harrass the Illinois, so that by 1714 the latter were practically driven away from their old homes on the Illinois never to return, having settled under the protecting arms of the French at Kaskaskia and Fort Chartres on the Mississippi. Indeed, the Foxes by their settlement on Fox river of Wisconsin and their destruction of the Illinois, had become virtual masters of both lines of travel between the east and the west, and communication between France and Louisiana became extremely difficult and dangerous. In fact, they had almost split the empire of New France asunder.

The situation had become desperate, therefore; and in 1716 De Louvingy was sent with eight hundred French and Indian allies to crush the

*HEBBERD: " *Wisconsin*," etc.
†PARKMAN: " *Half Century of Conflict.*"   ‡*Ibid.*

Foxes at their Wisconsin village. The latter were again badly punished, and gave hostages to preserve peace; but when, 1718, it appeared that but one of the hostages remained alive and he had lost an eye, the Foxes again became restless and soon began anew to harrass the Illinois tribes.*

At length the crisis came. The Illinois in 1722 captured the nephew of Oushala, the principal Fox war-chief, and burned him alive; on which the Foxes attacked them, drove them to the top of Starved Rock for refuge, and held them there at mercy. This Illinois tribe was the Peorias, the last of the tribes to cling to the famous stronghold of La Salle at Starved Rock, all the other tribes having fled to the west. "Unluckily we know nothing of the details of the siege, except the number of the slain: twenty Peorias and one hundred and twenty of the besiegers," says Hebberd.† "But the bare figures are eloquent; they tell not of a mere blockade, but of fierce assaults, storming parties, desperate attempts to scale the heights—the old story of Foxes' fury and reckless courage."

News of this attack on the Peorias having reached Fort Chartres, a detachment of a hundred men, commanded by Chevalier d'Artaguiette and Sieur de Tisne, was sent to their assistance. Before this reinforcement reached the Rock, however, the Foxes raised the siege and departed. The Peorias, nevertheless, abandoned their Illinois home, which they had occupied up to this time, and united with the other tribe at, Kaskaskia, so that after all the Foxes had been successful and again had control of the very heart of New France, the Illinois river.‡ "It was a grave disaster for the French," Charlevoix says; "for now that there is nothing to check the raids of the Foxes, communication between Canada and Louisiana became less practicable."§

At Versailles this last offense of the Foxes seemed unpardonable, and the colonial minister declared that "The Outagamies [Foxes] must be effect

---

* PARKMAN: "*Half Century of Conflict.*"
† HEBBERD: "*Wisconsin under the Dominion of France.*"
‡ BECKWITH: "*The Illinois and Indiana Indians.*"
§ CHARLEVOIX: "*History of New France.*" A famous traveler of the early 18th century.

ually put down, and that his Majesty will reward the officer who will reduce, or rather destroy, them."* In 1728, therefore, Sieur de Lignery went from Quebec with five hundred French and a thousand Indians to destroy the Foxes. In August, they burned the Indians' village in Wisconsin and destroyed their crops, but the nimble Foxes escaped him.

In 1730, Coulon de Villiers, who in 1754 defeated George Washington at Fort Necessity, appeared at Quebec with the news that his father, commander of the old Fort Miamis on St. Joseph river, had struck the Foxes a severe blow, killing two hundred of their warriors and six hundred women and children. Villiers' force of one hundred and seventy Frenchmen had been gathered from various western posts and was assisted by twelve to thirteen hundred Indian allies, under Sieurs de Saint-Ange, father and son, from the Illinois settlements, and De Noyelles, from among the Miamis in Indiana.

"The accounts of the affair are obscure and not very trustworthy," says Parkman.† "It seems that the Foxes began the fray by an attack on the Illinois at La Salle's old station of La Rocher [Starved Rock], on the river Illinois. On hearing of this the French commanders mustered their Indian allies, hastened to the spot, and found the Foxes intrenched in a grove which they had surrounded with a stockade."

"The battle began on the 19th of August, 1730, and lasted twenty-two days," says Hebberd,‡ who bases his account upon the narrative of Ferland.§ "The Foxes had chosen an admirable position in a piece of woods upon a gentle slope by the side of a small river. Although outnumbered four to one, they fought with their usual dash and valor, making many desperate sorties, but were each time driven back by the overwhelming numbers of the enemy. The French, on their part, dug trenches and proceeded with all the caution they had been taught by many campaigns against these redoubtable foes.

"After a while the supply of food gave out, and famine reigned in both camps. The Foxes and the French suffered alike under the calm, cruel im-

*PARKMAN : ' Half Century of Conflict."
†PARKMAN : Ibid.
‡HEBBERD : " Wisconsin," etc.
§FERLAND : "Cours d'Histoire du Canada."

partiality of nature. Two hundred Illinois Indians deserted. But the French persevered, and began the construction of a fort to prevent the besieged from going to the river for water. Further resistance now seemed impossible. But on the 8th of September a violent storm arose, accompanied by heavy thunder and torrents of rain. The following night was rainy, dark and cold; and under its cover the Foxes stole away from their fort. Before they had gone far the crying of their children betrayed them But the French did not dare to attack them amidst a darkness so dense that it was impossible to distinguish friend from foe. In the morning, however, they set out in hot pursuit."

The pursuit became a mere massacre (the Foxes being then without ammunition), from which only fifty or sixty of the Foxes escaped. Many of them were burned at the stake. And the Canadian governor's report to Paris closes with the cheering news: "Behold a nation humiliated in such a fashion that they will nevermore trouble the earth."

In truth "the offending tribe must now, one would think, have ceased to be dangerous," but nothing less than its total destruction would content the French.* The French, however, never afterwards sent an expedition against the Foxes, but turned them over to the tender mercies of their allies, especially the Hurons, their deadly enemies. But even they failed to annihilate these splendid savages, the remnant of whom allied themselves with the Sauks, a tribe who, as the Sauks and Foxes, were a continued menace to the frontier, and, in 1832, rose in open war with the United States authorities under their famous chief Black Hawk.

Though they met the fate of all their race, nevertheless the Foxes unconsciously, as has been seen, played an important part in shaping the destiny of the continent; for it was no slight service to liberty as opposed to absolutism that they closed the gateway between Canada and Louisiana and for thirty years virtually kept it closed, thus preventing the consolidation of New France and paving the way for the Anglo-Saxon conquest and occupation when the time was ripe for that happy event.

*PARKMAN: "'Half Century of Conflict."

Starved Rock, then, as the spot where took place the most important of those struggles between the French and their unconquerable savage foes, thus became a by no means insignificant part of the scenery of that greater contest of races and ideas which ultimately closed by "handing the continent over to its rightful inheritors, the freemen of America."

ROBERT CAVELIER SIEUR DE LA SALLE.
[Louis Hennepin's "Nouvelle Decouverte," London Edition of 1688. The picture is interesting, but as a portrait it has absolutely no value.]

STARVED ROCK, FROM THE EAST.

THE LIBRARY
OF THE
UNIVERSITY OF ILLINOIS

THE LAST OF THE ILLINOIS.

    Under the hollow sky,
Stretched on the prairie lone,
    Center of glory, I,
Bleeding, disdain to groan,
    But like a battle-cry
Peal forth my thunder moan.
    Baim—wah—wah!

    .   .   .   .

    Hark to those spirit notes!
Ye high heroes divine,
    Hymned from your god-like throats
That song of praise is mine!
    Mine, whose grave-pennon floats
O'er the foeman's line.
    Baim—wah - wah!
                —*Death Song.**

JUDGE CATON.

THE FINAL TRAGEDY.

IT is generally believed that the tragedy which gave Starved Rock its suggestive name was a part of the aftermath of the wars of the conspiracy of Pontiac; yet really authentic accounts of this occurrence are so few and of so uncertain authority that Beckwith† insists there is really no authority at all to support it, other than the "vague, though charming, traditions drawn from the wonder stories of many tribes." Yet no reader of this sketch will, I hope, be willing, however meagre our authority, to surrender, at Mr. Beckwith's dictum, so pa-

---

   * DEATH SONG: "*A be tuh ge zhig.*" Algonquin by Schoolcraft; English by C. F. Hoffman.
   † BECKWITH: "*Illinois and Indiana Indians.*"

thetic and picturesque a tale, hallowed as it is by the faith in its truth of our pioneer predecessors, who have woven the tale into the very fabric of local historical tradition. There is nothing in the least improbable in the legend; rather, there is much to support the affirmations of Indian, French and American traditions, that the tragedy of the obliteration by starvation here of a race of dusky warriors did actually take place as residents of the Illinois valley have been led to believe for at least seventy-five years.

It is not proposed to dwell on the Conspiracy of Pontiac. The student and the reader of romances alike will find the record in Parkman's volumes bearing that title: a broad historic projection for the student; history as charmingly told as romance for the general reader. Suffice it here to say, that a few days before his death, in 1769, Pontiac made his old friend, Pierre Chouteau, the trader, a visit at St. Louis; and while there heard of an Indian drinking bout or other festivities about to be held at Cahokia. Thither Pontiac went, in April, 1769, and while drunk, was, at the instigation of an Englishman, murdered, for the bribe of a barrel of whisky, by a Kaskaskia Indian.

The murder set the whole Illinois country aflame. "The news spread like lightning through the country," says one account, quoted by Parkman.* "The Indians assembled in great numbers, attacked and destroyed all the Peorias, except about thirty families, which were received into fort Chartres." All the authorities agree that the murder "brought on successive wars, and the almost total extermination of the Illinois." Parkman's own text says: "Could Pontiac's shade have revisited the scene of his murder, his savage spirit would have exulted in the vengeance which overwhelmed the abettors of the crime. Whole tribes were rooted out to expiate it. Chiefs and sachems, whose veins had thrilled with his eloquence; young warriors, whose aspiring hearts had caught the inspiration of his greatness, mustered to revenge his fate; and from the north and the east, their united bands descended on the villages of the Illinois. Tradition has but faintly preserved the memory of the event; and its only annalists, men who held the intestine

---

*PARKMAN: "*Conspiracy of Pontiac,*" Vol. II, p. 313—note.

THE FINAL TRAGEDY. 55

feuds of the savage tribes in no more account than the quarrels of panthers or wildcats, have left but a meagre record. Yet enough remains to tell us that over the grave of Pontiac more blood was poured out in atonement than flowed from the veins of the slaughtered heroes on the corpse of Patroclus; and the remnant of the Illinois who survived the carnage remained forever after sunk in utter insignificance."

The specific incident with which the name of Starved Rock is indissolubly linked is nowhere mentioned by the traveler s' tales or military reports of the time, nor are the Pottawatomie Indians named in connection with the revenge wreaked by Pontiac's Indian friends. Nevertheless, the Pottawatomie Indians, who had by this time come into possession of most of the lands in Illinois formerly held by the tribes who are named as a whole as the Illinois, were on the ground at this time, and without doubt took their part in the general fighting.

The "wonder story" which Mr. Beckwith cites as the most interesting of those preserving this tradition is that published by the late Judge Caton, in a pamphlet entitled, "The Last of the Illinois, and a Sketch of the Pottawatomies." The Judge in this sketch says that the wars against the Illinois tribes had so reduced them in numbers that now, in their direst extremity, driven hither as a last refuge, "they found sufficient space upon the half acre of ground which covers the summit of Starved Rock. As its sides are perpendicular, ten men could repel ten thousand with the means of warfare then at their command. The allies made no attempt to take the fort on the Rock by storm, but closely besieged it on every side. On the north, or river, side the upper rock overhangs the water somewhat, and tradition tells us how the confederates placed themselves in canoes under the shelving rock and cut the thongs of the besieged when they lowered their vessels to obtain water from the river, and so reduced them by thirst; but Meachelle,* as far I know, never mentioned this as one of the means resorted to by the confederates to reduce their enemies, nor, from an examination of the ground, do

---
* Meachelle was a Pottawatomie chief who told the story to Judge Caton, Meachelle being a boy at the time of the siege.

I think this probable; but they depended upon a lack of provisions, which we can readily appreciate must soon occur to a savage people who rarely anticipate the future in storing up supplies. How long the besieged held out Meachelle did not, and probably could not, tell us; but at last the time came when the unfortunate remnant could hold out no longer. They awaited but a favorable opportunity to attempt their escape. This was at last afforded by a dark and stormy night, when, led by their few remaining warriors, all stole in profound silence down the steep and narrow declivity to be met by a solid wall of their enemies surrounding the point where alone a sortie could be made, and which had been confidently expected. The horrid scene that ensued can be better imagined than described. No quarter was asked or given. For a time the howlings of the tempest were drowned by the yells of the combatants and the shrieks of the victims.

"Desperation lends strength to even enfeebled arms, but no efforts of valor could resist the overwhelming numbers actuated by the direst hate. The braves fell one by one, fighting like very fiends, and terribly did they revenge themselves upon their enemies. The few women and children, whom famine had left but enfeebled skeletons, fell easy victims to the war-clubs of the terrible savages, who deemed it as much a duty, and almost as great a glory, to slaughter the emaciated women and the helpless children as to strike down the men who were able to make resistance with arms in their hands. They were bent upon the utter extermination of their hated enemies, and most successfully did they bend their savage energies to the bloody task.

"Soon the victims were stretched upon the sloping ground south and west of the impregnable Rock, their bodies lying stark upon the sand which had been thrown up by the prairie winds. The wails of the feeble and the strong had ceased to fret the night winds, whose mournful sighs through the neighboring pines sounded like a requiem. Here was enacted the fitting finale to that work of death which had been commenced, scarcely a mile away, a century before by the still more savage and terrible Iroquois.

"Still, all were not destroyed. Eleven of the most athletic warriors, in the darkness and confusion of the fight, broke through the besieging lines.

LOOKING EAST FROM STARVED ROCK.

THE LIBRARY
OF THE
UNIVERSITY OF ILLINOIS

They had marked well from their high perch on the isolated Rock, the little nook below, where their enemies had moored at least a part of their canoes, and to these they rushed with headlong speed, unnoticed by their foes. In to these they threw themselves, and hurried down the rapids below. They had been trained to the use of the paddle and the canoe, and knew well every intricacy of the channel, so that they could safely thread it, even in the dark and boisterous night. They knew their deadly enemies would soon be in their wake, and that there was no safe refuge for them short of St. Louis. They had no provisions to sustain their waning strength, and yet it was certain death to stop by the way. Their only hope was in pressing forward by night and by day, without a moment's pause, scarcely looking back, yet ever fearing that their pursuers would make their appearance around the point they had last left behind. It was truly a race for life. If they could reach St. Louis, they were safe; if overtaken, there was no hope. We must leave to the imagination the details of a race where the stake was so momentous to the contestants. As life is sweeter even than revenge, we may safely assume that the pursued were impelled to even greater exertions than the pursuers. Those who ran for life won the race. They reached St. Louis before their enemies came in sight, and told their appalling tale to the commandant of the fort, from whom they received assurances of protection, and were generously supplied with food, which their famished condition so much required. This had barely been done when their enemies arrived and fiercely demanded their victims, that no drop of blood of their hated enemies might longer circulate in human veins. This was refused, when they retired with impotent threats of future vengeance, which they never had the means of executing.

"After their enemies had gone, the Illinois, who never after even claimed that name, thanked their entertainers, and, full of sorrow which no words can express, slowly paddled their way across the river, to seek new friends among the tribes who then occupied the southern part of this state, and who would listen with sympathy to the sad tale they had to relate. They alone remained the broken remnant and last representatives of their once great nation. Their name, even now, must be blotted out from among the names of the aboriginal tribes. Henceforth they must cease to be of the present, and could only be remembered as a part of the past. This is the last we know of the last of the Illinois. They were once a great and prosperous people, as advanced and as humane as any of the aborigines around them; we do not know that a drop of their blood now animates a human being, but their name is perpetuated in this great state, of whose record of the past all of us feel so proud, and of whose future the hopes of us all are so sanguine.

"Till the morning light revealed that the canoes were gone the confederates believed that their sanguinary work had been so thoroughly done that not a living soul remained. So soon as the escape was discovered, the pursuit was commenced, but as we have seen, without success. The pursuers returned disappointed and dejected that their enemies' scalps were not hanging from their belts. But surely blood enough had been spilled—vengeance should have been more than satisfied.

"I have failed, no doubt, to properly render Meachelle's account of this sad drama, for I have been obliged to use my own language, without the inspiration awakened in him by the memory of the scene which served as his first baptism in blood. Who can wonder that it made a lasting impression on his youthful mind? Still, he was not fond of relating it, nor would he speak of it except to those who had acquired his confidence and intimacy. It is probably the only account to be had related by an eye-witness, and we may presume that it is the most authentic."

While the writer must confess that the learned and venerable jurist's version of the Starved Rock tradition is open to the criticism that some of its details seem improbable, nevertheless of the substantial truth of the legend, we believe there can be but little doubt. Even man's wonder stories have always something of fact, of human experience, or of physical phenomena behind them, as one might reply to Mr. Beckwith's skepticism. But the story of Starved Rock, as told by Judge Caton, has been corroborated by other competent searchers for truth, especially by Hon. Perry A. Armstrong, of Morris, one of the pioneers of Illinois, who knew personally many of the famous Indians of this part of the state who died subsequently to the coming of the permanent American settlers. Among these was an old chief named Shick Shack, claiming to be 104 years of age, who, as Mr. Armstrong said, in an address* at a celebration at Starved Rock, of the two-hundredth anniversary (September 10, 1873) of its discovery, told him substantially the same story that Meachelle told Judge Caton, which the latter published in 1876. Shick Shack said he was present at the siege, a boy half grown.

The late N. Matson,† of Princeton, was another student of this legend. In prosecuting his historical researches, he spent much time (prior to 1882) with the descendants of old French colonists who had lived at Kaskaskia and Cahokia in the last century. Mr. Matson was more than convinced of the truth of the legend, so-called. Indeed, he goes so far as to identify "the only survivor of the fearful tragedy." This warrior, Mr. Matson tells us, was a young man, "partly white, being a descendant on his father's side from the French. Being alone in the world after the catastrophe, he went to Peoria, joined the colony, and there ended his days. He embraced Christianity," Mr. Matson continues, "and became an officer in the church, assuming the name of Antonio La Bell; and his descendants are now (1882) living near Prairie du Rocher [on the Mississippi], one of whom, Charles La Bell, was a party to a suit in the United States court to recover the land on which Peoria now stands."

Mr. Matson further states that Col. Jos. N. Bourassa, a descendant of the Illinois French, living (1882) in Kansas, had collected a large number of stories relating to the Starved Rock tragedy; and himself had heard two aged warriors, who participated in the massacre, narrate many incidents which took place at that time. Another old Indian named Mashaw, once well known by early Ottawa and Hennepin traders, Mr. Matson says, also made various statements, through an interpreter, in relation to the tragedy, to early American traders and settlers. Mashaw said that seven Indians escaped from the Rock Medore Jennette, also, an employe of the Chouteaus, the famous fur traders at St. Louis, who lived many years at an Indian vil-

---
*Ottawa Free Trader, September, 1873.
† MATSON: "Pioneers of Illinois." 1882.

lage at the mouth of Fox river, has left many traditions of this tragedy to his descendants, according to Mr. Matson. Jennette came to the country in 1772 and says he himself saw the bones of the dead Illinois upon the Rock. An Indian named Shaddy (or Shaty) was still another who gave Mr. Matson details of this story, which he had from his father, who was present. Shaddy (Shaty) said only one man, the half-breed La Bell, escaped. Two traders, Robert Maillet and Felix La Pance, are said to have left the record that, returning from Canada with goods, they saw the buzzards on Starved Rock cleaning the bones of the dead. Further, Mr. Matson adds that Father Buche, a priest of Peoria, traveling up Illinois river the following spring (1770), ascended the Rock and there saw the horrid evidences of the tragedy, the holy Father's written story of this visit being in manuscript (dated April, 1770), which, in 1882, was in the hands of one Hypolite Pilette, then living on the American Bottom.

Not to go further, it may be said in conclusion that there is nothing improbable in the Starved Rock legend. Speaking of the remorseless massacre of several hundred Foxes (Outagamies) at Detroit, 1712, by French and Indians, Dr. Parkman* says : " There is a disposition to assume that events like that just recounted were a consequence of the contact of white men with red, but the primitive Indian was quite able to enact such tragedies without the aid of Europeans. Before French or English influence had been felt in the interior of the continent, a great part of North America was the frequent witness of scenes more lurid in coloring and on a larger scale of horror. In the first half of the seventeenth century the whole country, from Lake Superior to the Tennessee and from the Alleghenies to the Mississippi, was ravaged by wars of extermination, in which tribes, large and powerful, by Indian standards, perished, dwindled into feeble remnants or were absorbed by other tribes and vanished from sight." Extermination by red man's and white man's hands alike was the fate of the Indian; and the Starved Rock tragedy was but an incident of the resistless and remorseless movement of Indian destiny.

---

*PARKMAN : *"Half Century of Conflict."*

CANYON SOUTH OF STARVED ROCK.

THE SEQUEL.

Far as we are informed, so thick and fast they fell,
Scarce twenty of their number at night did get home well.
—*Puritan Ballad.*

THE POTTAWATOMIES.

THE Hon. P. A. Armstrong, of Morris, Ill., who has written much upon the Indian wars of Illinois during this century, in 1873 published in the Morris *Reformer* a series of articles on the Starved Rock tradition, based upon personal interviews had sixty years ago with early pioneers of La Salle and Grundy counties, as well as the retiring red men, trappers, traders and other frontiersmen. After sketching the war which ended with the Rock tragedy, Mr. Armstrong brings the conquering tribes together the following spring on Indian Creek, in La Salle county, north and east of Ottawa, where they met to have a jollification over their victory, and then proceeds substantially as follows:

"On this occasion weeks were spent in feasting, dancing and merry-making,—weeks fraught with the most direful consequences to the peace and harmony of the allies; for at this feast each and every warrior was allowed and expected to recite in the most exaggerated manner his prowess as a warrior; the scalps he had taken, the dangers encountered and sufferings endured, commencing in all instances with 'Big Indian me.' Jealousies at once sprung up as each candidate applied for applause, the squaws and pappooses naturally siding with the warriors of their respective tribes, and a feeling of distrust, if not hate, was soon engendered, which daily increased, so that when the chiefs came to talk about the division of the territory they had acquired, each tribe claimed the lion's share.

"Of the territory west of the Illinois river they knew nothing, and they all desired that territory watered by the Illinois river and its tributaries. An amicable division or adjustment could not be made. The Miamis were by far more numerous than either of the other tribes, and moreover were much better armed, since they had quite a number of muskets while the other tribes had none This rendered the Miamis very domineering and haughty. They demanded all or nearly all of the newly acquired territory, which, of course, the other two tribes resisted; hence an open rupture was made, and a battle ensued upon the very grounds they had used in feasting, the Pottawatomies and Kickapoos uniting their forces against the Miamis. Many were slain on both sides; and after fighting from morning until night, the Miamis took advantage of the night to withdraw, leaving the allies in possession of the battle field. But this battle, although a severe one, was by no means a decisive one. The losses on both sides were heavy, and neither were in a condition to renew the fight for several months, as they were out of provisions and short of clothing and implements of war.

"The balance of the summer and following winter were spent in preparing for a renewal of the contest the following spring. The Miamis went down the river and thence to Kaskaskia, while the Pottawatomies and Kickapoos remained near their previous winter quarters, collecting provisions and clothing, and constructing bows and arrows and other implements of Indian warfare. Early in the spring following (1771), the Miamis returned northward to give battle to their late allies, but now bitter enemies, and were met near Peoria, where another battle was fought, which, like the former one, was not decisive—was, indeed, a drawn battle; and each party buried their own dead. The evidences of these two great battles are (1873) still visible in the numerous mounds where they buried their dead, which are still there to mark the spot; and arrow flints and other implements of Indian warfare have been found in the neighborhood by the bushel.

"The war lasted, with indifferent success to either party, for about five years, and many a hard fought battle attested the bravery of these unfortunate, passion-blinded savages, who left their dead buried in many places throughout the coveted territory. In the year 1775 they had worked around and nearly back to the place where their first battle had occurred with the Illini. Harassed and worn by excessively long marches and repeated and sanguinary battles, both armies were well nigh exhausted.

"A proposition was then made on the part of the Miamis to pick three hundred warriors from each side and let them commence to fight at sunrise and continue the fight until either the one side or the other should conquer This proposition was at once accepted by the Pottawatomies and Kickapoos, upon the condition that the weapons on both sides should be the bow and arrow, tomahawk, knife and spear, or such implements of warfare as were peculiarly Indian, and that the remnant of each army should cross to the east side of the Wabash river, so that no assistance or interference could possibly be made by either side. This agreement was entered into with all the solemnity of the high councils of these respective tribes, and three hundred picked warriors were selected from each side, who crossed over to the bloody ground and encamped upon Sugar Creek, which empties into the Wabash river. The place selected for this terrible duel was a heavy timber about twenty miles from the Wabash. The battle was to commence at sunrise the following morning.

"The fated morning came—a calm, cool, bright September morn, and with the coming of the morning sun the battle commenced. Six hundred stalwart warriors engaging in a strife for victory or death.

"They practiced every pass and word
To thrust, to strike, to feint, to guard.

"Here were the deeds of a Thermopylæ re-enacted. Quarter was neither asked nor given—'death was the watchword and reply.' Now shielding behind some giant oak—every ruse was resorted to in the hope of inducing the enemy to expose his person—now grappling in a death struggle, the combatants fell never to rise again.

"This duel raged from sunrise to sunset, when twelve warriors only remained—five Miamis and seven Pottawatomies and Kickapoos. The five run, the seven are the victors. The great chiefs, Shick Shack, Sugar, Marquett and Shaty were among the seven. The Miamis were conquered; and by their agreement gave up all claim to the hunting ground of the annihilated Illini and retired east of the Wabash.

"Thus did the Pottawattomies and Kickapoos become the successors of the Illini, and soon after this final battle with the Miamis they divided the territory between themselves, the Kickapoos taking all the territory adjoining the Wabash west to a line running north and south through Oliver's Grove in Livingston county, and the Pottawatomies all the territory west of that line."

The Pottawatomies having taken undisputed possession of their conquest, made their principal village on the plain northwest of Starved Rock, near the present village of Utica, where, among others, the youthful G. S. Hubbard, later one of the founders of the city of Chicago, as representative of the American Fur Company, carried on a trade with them. Here, unlike the vanished Illini, the Pottawatomies lived in tents, not in cabins. Another important village was called Waubunsee (or Wauponehsee), located at the mouth of the Pish-ta-ka (or Poish-tah-le koosh : antelope), as these Indians called the Fox river of Illinois, and the ancient city of Ottawa.

In 1814, however, a treaty was made with the Ottawas, Chippewas and Pottawatomies, kindred tribes, by Ninian Edwards, William Clark and Auguste Chouteau, by which the Indians gave up their Illinois lands south of a line running west from Lake Michigan to the Mississippi. A few years later (1834) the Pottawatomies were removed from Illinois to new lands beyond the Mississippi; and the Indian's part in the history of Starved Rock came to an end forever.

MODERN STARVED ROCK.

> Methinks you take luxurious pleasure
> In your novel western leisure.
> —*Thoreau.*

THE ERA OF THE WHITE MAN.

"THEN the white man came, pale as the dawn, with a load of thought, with slumbering intelligence as a fire raked up. He bought the Indian's moccasins and furs; then he bought his hunting grounds; and at length he forgot where the Indian was buried and plowed up his bones." The tale is soon told; for it is but a variation of the theme which but now is dying away in the west, as the Indian slowly disappears off the face of the earth. And from a feudal castle of Sieur de la Salle and a Rock of Refuge for hunted savages, Starved Rock has passed into its "western leisure."

Always a landmark of the great West in the more important epochs of its history, it still was such when the English settlers began to invade the Illinois country; and it would be difficult to find a traveler journeying in the Illinois valley "spying out the land," who has not told of going out of his way to visit and call attention to this remarkable natural curiosity. Flint in his "History and Geography of the Mississippi Valley," published in 1833, devotes a page to "Rock Fort," describing the beauty of the Rock itself and its surroundings and repeating the tradition that has given it its name, though Flint nowhere calls it other than "Rock Fort." Chas. Fenno Hoffman, a then distinguished New York author and *litterateur*, who visited the Rock in January, 1834, while on a winter tour through the West, on the other hand, calls the place "Starved Rock" and nothing else, showing that such was its common name at that time in the Illinois country. Hoffman has a note, written by an unidentified friend resident in Illinois, which repeats the familiar legend, with this single exception, that while the writer says one person escaped from the Rock, that person was a squaw, who was still alive when the Englishmen entered the country. Schoolcraft (1820), in his "Travels through the Central Portions of the Mississippi Valley," records having visited the Rock, when he made the sketch from which the engraving used as initial to this chapter has been made. Judge Hall's (Ohio) "Tales of the Border" (183-), also contains the Starved Rock legend, which was the common property of all western travelers of that early day.

Of all the many articles that were written of Starved Rock in the past, however, none, perhaps, came to have a wider circulation, or gave the Rock wider celebrity, than one written by Charles Lanman, an article erroneously attributed by some of our more celebrated local historians to Washington Irving, who unfortunately, so far as I have been able to discover, never saw and certainly never wrote a line about the Rock. The article seems to have been Mr. Lanman's "swan song," but having been published as an "elegant extract in prose from an eloquent writer" in the famous "Sanders Series" of readers (my copy is edition of 1855), "for the use of academies and the higher classes in common and select schools," it was read and declaimed by the youth of that and succeeding decades from one end of the nation to the other; and I have no doubt that the article so published has been the means of bringing thousands of curious visitors to the Rock in the past forty years.

The era of the "plowshare and pruning hook" has come to Starved Rock. "Grim-visaged war hath smoothed his wrinkled front," and the frightful and laborious past, soothed and softened by the tempering touch of lapsing time, has left its record, which now is like the

> Legends and runes
> Of credulous days; old fancies that have lain
> Silent from boyhood, taking voice again,
> Warmed into life once more, even as tunes
> That, frozen in the fabled hunting horn,
> Thawed into sound.

The modern Starved Rock beleaguerers come arrayed in bicycle suits and picnic habiliments; and where once the Frenchman braved the terrors of savagery, his nineteenth century successors, born of all nations, now invade the land to make an *al fresco* holiday.

To-day, too, its Kaskaskia cabins have been replaced by a modern hotel, with broad verandas, an attractive dining room, and large and airy guest chambers, supplied with water, gas, and the comforts of a hotel of the best class, and with private cottages attached for families,—many comforts which, to the Rock's earliest master, Louis the Magnificent, would have been impossible luxuries. The broad verandas overlook the verdant, peaceful valley, while the cool shade of the forest but a step to the rear of the hotel brings rest and refreshment to the tired worker seeking here summer rest and recreation for renewed exertion in the business world. Separated from the hotel is a club house where dancing parties are held; and again the sound of music and merry laughter,—that once without doubt echoed from the summit of the Rock in the ancient days when the pleasure-loving Frenchmen found themselves at peace with savage foes,—is caught up by the sweet south wind to fill again the quiet valley with the harmonies of peace and happiness.

Near by, and accessible to pleasure seekers, are the cliffs, the glens and the canyons of Illinois river, which unite to make this the most interesting locality from a scenic point of view on the entire stream. Farther away, but still within even walking distance—a few miles—are the famous Bailey's Falls and Deer Park Glen, the beauty spots of the Big Vermilion river, which itself is for many miles of its length the most interesting region, from the geologist's and artist's point of view, in all northern Illinois. Deer Park Glen has been greatly beautified of late years by the creation of roads and paths and by the removal of the refuse of nature; but here, as is also the policy of the Starved Rock management, not one jot or tittle of nature's own beauty or handiwork has been or will be disturbed.

Of all this interesting region the Starved Rock Hotel is the natural center; and its management offers its guests all facilities for examining every portion of the region at their leisure. The Hotel, owned by Walther & Huehl, of Chicago, and managed (1895) by Wm. Tatsch, is the equal in all respects of the best summer hotels of the West; and thus Starved Rock is rapidly becoming the most popular summer resort in the Illinois valley, its register during the past few years having contained names of visitors from nearly every state of the Union.

STARVED ROCK HOTEL, FROM TOP OF THE ROCK.

THE LIBRARY
OF THE
UNIVERSITY OF ILLINOIS

THE HISTORIANS.

> As year by year his tapestry unrolled,
>   What varied wealth its growing length displayed!
>   What long processions flamed in cloth of gold!
>   What stately forms the flowing robes arrayed!
>
> He told the red man's story ; far and wide
>   He searched the unwritten records of his race.
> —*Oliver Wendell Holmes.*

FRANCIS PARKMAN.

DR. FRANCIS PARKMAN, born in Boston, September 16 1823, came of an ancestry distinguished for scholarly attainment and achievement; and so early was his own taste and aptitude for literature disclosed that in 1840, at the age of seventeen, he was meditating on a history of the French and Indian wars, or, to be more specific, the "History of France and England in North America." This project took definite shape, and from boyhood to the end the work of a lifetime was pursued with exceptional consistency and inspiring steadfastness of aim and endeavor. It was practically fifty years from the time he began his life's work to the day he completed it—by an interesting coincidence naming his last volume, "Fifty Years of Conflict."

"The Oregon Trail," which was a prelude to his great undertaking, was the result of a summer journey, undertaken by himself and his cousin, Quincy A. Shaw, in 1846, across the continent into the Black Hills. As Dr. Parkman's nearest friend, Rev. Julius H. Ward,* has said : "This volume shows how he became acquainted with the kind of life which in writing of the early settlement of North America he was called upon to describe. It laid the foundation of the attractive interest and the feeling of reality which

---

* See *The Outlook*, 1893.

FRANCIS PARKMAN, LL.D.

are everywhere imparted to his narrative. Mr. Parkman entered into his undertaking with such ardor and enthusiasm that, before he was aware of it, he had overtaxed his strength and had prepared the way for permanent physical infirmity—not that of eyesight, except to a limited extent, but a tendency to congestion of the brain, which all his life withdrew him from the field of active duty and constantly interfered with his work as a scholar, now reaching him in disability of this organ and now in the infirmity of that, and constantly limiting him in his hours of work and compelling him to go at a snail's pace when he felt as if the only satisfaction to his spirit would have been to march forward like a colonel at the head of his regiment. His physical infirmities were a tremendous drawback in his life-work, but his spirit was so resolute, and he lived so much above his limitations of body, that nothing interfered with his great object, and he lived to complete his work and bring the history down to the year 1760, when the English completed their conquest of New France, and to see the plan which he laid out while a college student developed and treated in every respect as exhaustively as the materials will permit."

"The Oregon Trail" is an incomparable picture of the life that once existed on the great plains of the Far West, which has now disappeared forever. It was dictated to his traveling companion; and all his life thereafter he was dependent on the pens of his friends or of paid amanuenses not only for the performance of the labor of writing his words at his dictation, but for the collection and collating of materials under his direction. Five times he went to Europe, taking with him trained assistants to aid him in procuring the necessary data for his histories. Tens of thousands of maps and folio copies of documents were made in the museums and public archives of France and England. With infinite patience and labor all of these were examined, in order that the histories might cover every important detail of their time with absolute accuracy.

In 1850 he married Catherine Bigelow, and for a brief space (less than eight years) found in her companionship sweet solace for an illness which to a lesser man would have been a veritable death in life. Yet these were the happiest years of his life.

In 1851 the "Conspiracy of Pontiac" appeared, the first of that notable series of historical narratives entitled "France and England in America," though chronologically it is the last.

Not again until 1858, after the death of his wife, did Dr. Parkman find physical strength to resume his life's work. In the meantime, as a diversion, he essayed the role of a novelist, "Vassall Morton" being his third book. "It was a *succes d'estime.*" But "the man who could make history more fascinating than romance, saw that it was a waste of time and talents to make novels less agreeable than history; and he never repeated the experiment."

In spite of the fact that for some years he could do absolutely nothing; that for many more he could work but five minutes a day, and that he never was able to work above ten hours, or to compose above five hundred words a day, his purpose never faltered; but the successive volumes came slowly, "The Pioneers of France in the New World" (1865); "The Jesuits in North America" (1867); "La Salle and the Discovery of the Great West" (1869); "The Old Regime in Canada" (1874); "Count Frontenac and New France" (1877); "Montcalm and Wolfe" (1884); and "A Half Century of Conflict" (1892)—with which last the author laid down his pen (dying November 8, 1893), a life task fulfilled—fulfilled with the happiness of complete recognition of its significance and uniqueness, and with the world's acknowledgement that never need the work be repeated.

"The twelve volumes which constitute the history as it now stands," as Dr. Ward remarks, "constitute a work which has a permanent value. It is a thorough examination of all the facts and an impartial treatment of them. This has been conceded by Catholic and Protestant students. It is as free from excess in one direction as in the other. Mr. Parkman is able to sympathize with both parties in the contention for the mastery of North America, and usually allows the facts to speak for themselves and lead us to their obvious conclusion. It is these qualities of thoroughness and impartiality which give his work authority, and the charming style in which it is written insures a permanent popularity."

His publishers, Little, Brown & Co., Boston, have recently issued a new edition of his works, with his latest revisions, including "The Oregon Trail," characteristically illustrated by Frederick Remington. The edition is superior in workmanship, convenient in size and moderate in price.

JOHN GILMARY SHEA, LL.D.

Thou thy worldly task hast done,
Home art gone and ta'en thy wages.
— *Anon*

JOHN GILMARY SHEA, LL.D.

After Parkman, no one man, perhaps, has done more to recover the history of the early French in the Mississippi valley than Dr Shea. Deeply religious by nature and early training, and, after his graduation from Columbia College, of which his father was a professor, for six years a novice of the Society of Jesus, he became as a Catholic much interested in the early history of Catholicism on this continent, and was especially moved, as must be every imaginative mind, by the heroism of the men who first carried the cross to the Indians of the St. Lawrence and Great Lakes valleys.

Compelled by precarious health to abandon the university, he resumed the practice of law, interrupted by his connection with the Jesuits; but his historical studies, one may imagine, consumed much of the time other lawyers would have given to their briefs His preliminary literary work was in the form of contributions to Catholic periodicals, which quickly brought him to the attention of the literary world, especially of historical students of this country and Europe. At the age of twenty-six (1850), he published his "History of the Discovery and Exploration of the Mississippi River," a work whose apparent great research in the buried archives of Canadian governmental and sacerdotal records, and whose accuracy and uniqueness, at once placed him in the rank of the first rate historians of his country. It was the first work to give dignity and form to an important part of our western annals. It has been honored and approved by frequent reference by Dr. Parkman.

An equally, and perhaps in some respects even more, important service was the editing and publishing by him of twenty six volumes of the missionaries' "Relations" (official reports), all of which were outside and in addition to those published by the Canadian government, covering the early French explorations in the great West and invaluable as a mine for original research. His "History of the Catholic Missions among the Indian Tribes of the United States" is also a monument to his learning, industry and piety. Both of these works are deeply interesting to the student of to-day.

He was an indefatigable worker, and a list of his books and contributions to periodicals and historical society records would fill a goodly page. His last and perhaps greatest work was a "History of the Catholic Church in the United States," which he finished on his death-bed.

As to his work in generally, Dr. Richard H. Clark, in the "Catholic

Family Annual,"* truly says: "His position in the special department of Catholica Americana was unequalled and unique. His advent in our midst at a time when our Catholic historical records and materials were wasting was providential, for he was foremost in teaching us their value and in making a noble and able use of them. He was by prestige in his day the historian of the American Catholic Church." And, it may be added, he was also a man in whom the Christian virtues which adorned his private life were covered by a veil of modesty and humility.

He was born in New York July 22, 1824; and died at Elizabeth, N. J., February 22, 1892.

MRS. MARY H. CATHERWOOD.

Give to barrows, trays and pans,
Grace and glimmer of romance. — *Emerson*.

THE NOVELIST.

MRS. CATHERWOOD.

Mrs. Mary Hartwell Catherwood, a resident of Hoopestown, Illinois, in "The Romance of Dollard," "The Story of Tonty," etc., has in romance done for the period of French dominion in North America what Parkman has done for it in history: recreated the period for the instruction and amusement of present generations; and if Parkman has given to history the charm of romance, Mrs. Catherwood has no less served history by reproducing in romance the charm of local color, in the realistic pictures of the life of the Canadian and Illinois people of those far-away days, without which history itself is incomplete and unsatisfactory.

* I am indebted to this book for the materials of this imperfect sketch, as well as for the original of the portrait of Dr. Shea herewith.

The reader of this sketch is the more interested in "The Story of Tonty," since the characters of the tale are the heroes of Starved Rock, while the Rock itself is the scene of not the least absorbing events of the story.

"The Story of Tonty" is the story of a friend. The most faithful of servants, Tonty was also the most steadfast of friends—that rarest of human blessings, which at best comes to a few men only, and to each but once. Parkman has borne testimony to the disinterested fidelity of Tonty; but it remained for Mrs. Catherwood in "The Story of Tonty" to recreate the living man and present him to us crowned with the praises of "historians, priests, tradition, savages and his own deeds."

The story opens with the "Beaver Fair" at Montreal, 1678. La Salle and Tonty had just arrived from France to explore the West. The picture of the savage gathering assembled for trade and a pow-wow with Frontenac, the governor, is very realistic. The thread of enmity against La Salle that appears in the conversations of the traders and merchants is a hint of his ultimate failure, and discloses also the reasons for it. In Book II the scene is La Salle's Lake Ontario fort, Ft. Frontenac; and the theme is La Salle's earlier disappointments and the adverse influences operating against him on the St. Lawrence. In Book III the scene is at Starved Rock during that distressing period when La Salle was in France for the last time; was murdered in Texas, and when his brother and Joutel, saved from the fate of La Salle, enjoying Tonty's hospitality, hid from him the news of the death of his master and friend, La Salle.

The story is faithful to the thread of La Salle's career, and so is full of heroism and suffering, deception and treachery, "envy, hatred and malice and all uncharitableness," relieved, however, by the loving faithfulness of Barbe, La Salle's niece, and Tonty, his friend. Nearly all the celebrated names in northwestern discovery in the seventeenth century are met in the course of the story; which completes, with its color, the picture, the drawing of which was the work of Parkman, the historian.

NOTE.—I am indebted to the courtesy of A. C. McClurg & Co., publishers of "The Story of Tonty," for the portrait of Mrs. Catherwood herewith.

ENTRANCE TO DEER PARK GLEN.

**THE LIBRARY
OF THE
UNIVERSITY OF ILLINOIS**

RELICS.

Some rusted swords appear in dust;
One, bending forward, says,
"The arms belonged to heroes gone;
We never hear their praise in song."
—*Duan of Ca-Lodin.*

THE SILENT WITNESSES.

ON the bluff about twenty-four hundred feet south of Starved Rock, at the junction of two ravines, as shown by the map on the following page the faint and disappearing remains may be said to be still visible of an old earthwork of irregular shape. The map*—made, I believe, from a survey by Col. D. F. Hitt, for many years the owner of Starved Rock, having had his deed directly from the United States government—indicates its form and size. Much learned conjecture, not omitting, of course suitable reference to the Aztecs and dates not long subsequent to the Noachian period, has been put on paper touching the origin of this so called fort, which even the French are credited with having built, though its usefulness to them can hardly be conjectured; but the truth seems to be that it is the remains of a stockade, perhaps, erected by the Shawanoe Indians when they resided there as a part of La Salle's famous settlement of 1682-3. A reference to the Franquelin map (page 30) shows the location of two hundred cabins of the Chaouenon at the point where these remains are found. La Salle, says Parkman, "undoubtedly supplied Franquelin with materials" for this map. And Parkman also says: "The Shawanoe camp, or village, is placed on the south side of the river, behind the fort (Starved Rock). The country here is hilly, broken, and now, as in La Salle's time, covered with wood,

---
*Reproduced (reduced size) from "*Baldwin's History of La Salle County.*"

which, however, soon ends in the open prairie. The village of the Shawanoes on Franquelin's map corresponds with the position of this earthwork."

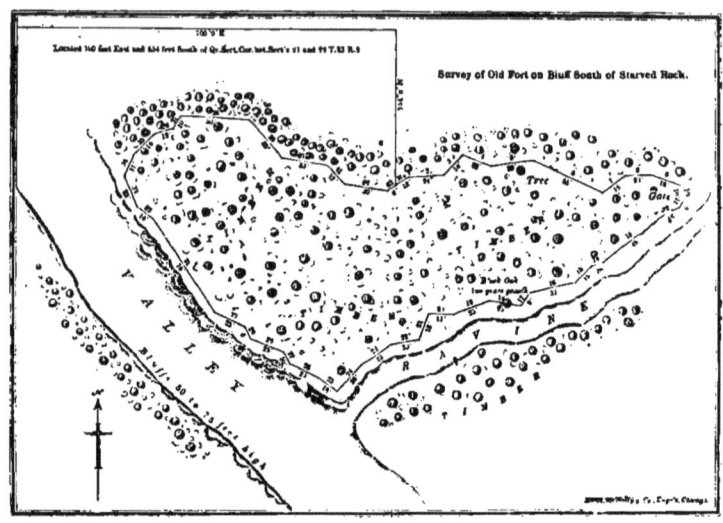

AN ANCIENT DEED.

[TRANSLATION.]

"The year 1693, the 19th of April, I, Francis de la Forest, Captain on the retired list in the marine service, Seignor of part of all the country of Louisiana, otherwise Illinois, granted to Monsieur de Tonty and to me by the King to enjoy in perpetuity, we, our heirs. successors, and assigns, the same as it was recognized by the act of the Sovereign Council in Quebec in the month of August, of the year 1691, the said council assembled, declare in the presence of the undersigned witness that I have ceded, sold, and transferred to Mr. Michel Acau* the half of my part of the above described concession, to enjoy the same like myself from the present time, to him, his heirs, successors, and assigns, with the same rights, privileges, prerogatives and benefits

---

*See chapter on "The Missions," supra.

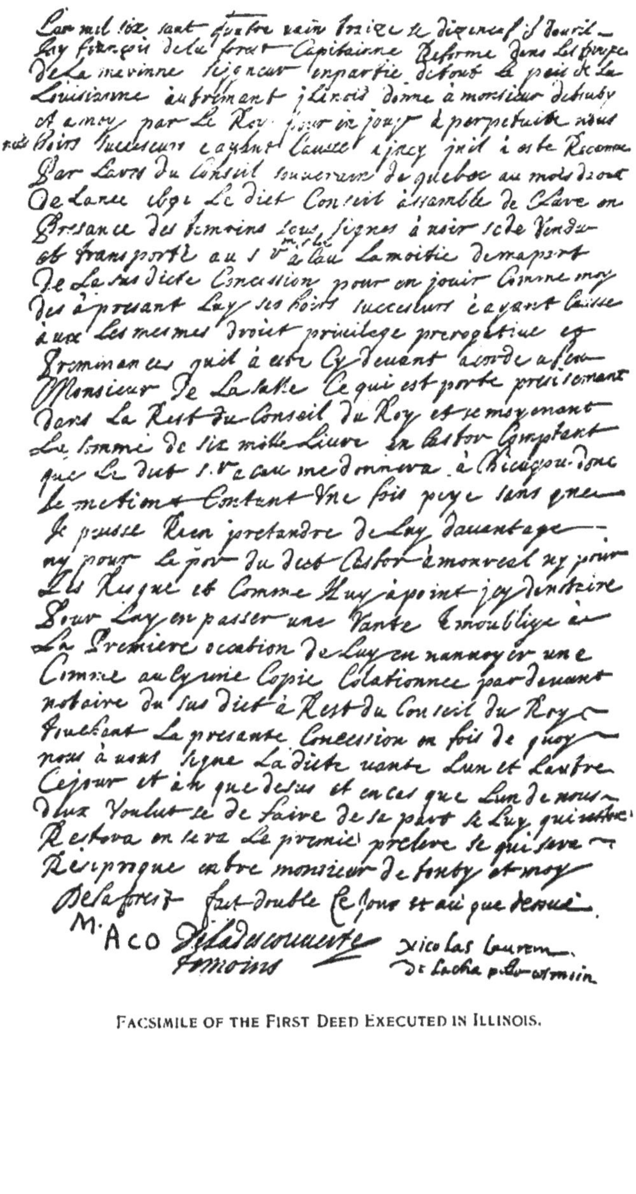

Lan mil six sant quatre vain treize le dixneuf d'avril —
Lay françois delu forest Capitaine Reforme dans les troupes
De la marinne seigneur enpartie detout le pais de la
Louisianne autrement ilinois donne a monsieur detunty
et a moy par le Roy pour en jouy a perpetuite nous
nos hoirs successeurs e ayant cause e jcey quil a este Reconnu
par Larest du Conseil souuerain de quebec au mois deout
De lannee 1692 Le dict Conseil assamble de Clare en
presance des temoins sous signes a uoir cede Vendu
et transporte au s michle acclau lamoitie demapart
De la sus dicte Concession pour en jouir comme moy
des a present luy ses hoirs successeurs e ayant caisse
aux les mesmes droict privilege prerogative et
preminances quil a este cy deuant acorde a feu
Monsieur de la Salle ce qui est porte precisemant
dans la Rest du Conseil du Roy et se moyenant
La somme de six mille Livre en castor comptant
que le dit s acau me donnera a chicagou dont
le metiems content une fois peye sans que
Je pusse Rien pretandre de luy dauantage
ny pour le por du dict castor a monreal ny pour
les risque et comme il ny a point jcy denotaire
pour luy en passer une vante je moubliye a
la premiere ocation de luy en nanvoyer une
comme aussy une copie colationnee par deuant
notaire du sus dict a rest du conseil du Roy
touchant la presante concession en fois de quoy
nous auons signe la dicte vante lun et lautre
Cejour et an que dessus et en cas que lun de nous
deux voulut se de faire de sa part se luy qui restra
Restera on sera le premie prefere se qui sera
Reciproque entre monsieur de tonty et moy
De la forest fait double ce jour et an que dessus.
M. Aco Deladescouuerte
temoins
Nicolas Laurem
de Lacha

FACSIMILE OF THE FIRST DEED EXECUTED IN ILLINOIS.

which have been heretofore accorded to the late M. de la Salle as it appears particularly in the decree of the Council of the King; and in considerntion of the sum of 6,000 livres in current beaver which the said Mr. Acau shall pay me at Chicagou, where I stay, and upon the making of the payment down I cannot demand from him any advantage neither for the carriage of the said beaver to Montreal nor for the risk, and as there is no notary here for him to pass an instrument of sale I bind myself at the first occasion to send him one, as also a copy compared before a notary of the above mentioned decree of the Council of the King touching the present concession, on faith of which we have both signed the said contract of sale the one and the other the day and the year as above; and in case that one of us two would dispose of his part the remaining one shall be the first preferred, and this is mutual between M. de Tonty and me. Made in duplicate the day and year aforesaid.

"DE LA FOREST. DE LA DESCOUVERTES, Witness.

"M. ACO. NICOLAS LAURENS, DE LA CHAPELLE, Witness."

The deed is indorsed on the back to the following effect : "Bill of sale between Mr. Ako and me conveying the land of the Illinois."

This deed was purchased in Paris, late in year 1893, by Hon. Edward G. Mason and deposited by him in the archives of the Historical Society of Chicago, January 16, 1894. It is believed to be the first conveyance of Illinois real estate,—though how much or where it lay is not very clear, except that it was the Illinois country,—made by deed executed within the borders of this state. The document covers one page of large foolscap paper and is apparently all in the handwriting of La Forest. The paper bears an ancient watermark and is of the same texture and quality as that used in Canada at the time of its date.

In presenting the document to the Society, Mr. Mason epitomized the facts given in this little book, concluding as follows :

"The grantee in the deed, whose name is usually written Michel Accau, was the real leader of the party which, by La Salle's direction, explored the Upper Mississippi and discovered the falls of St. Anthony in 1682. Father Hennepin accompanied this expedition as a volunteer, and [having written an account of his travels on that occasion] is usually given the credit of its discoveries. Accau subsequently resided in Kaskaskia [Starved Rock] and married a daughter of the chief of the Kaskaskia tribe. A record of their marriage still exists in the ancient register of the [new] parish of the Immaculate Conception at Kaskaskia [on the Mississppi].

"Of the witnesses, De La Descouverte was a Canadian voyageur from Lachine, who accompanied La Salle to the mouth of the Mississippi in 1682, and La Chapelle was also one of La Salle's men who was with him in the year 1680, and was sent by him from the St. Joseph River and the Michillimackinac in search of La Salle's lost vessel, the *Griffin*, and afterwards joined Tonty at Fort Creve-Cœur, near the present site of Peoria.

"It is quite certain that this document was executed either at Fort St. Louis of the Illinois or at Chicago, with the probability in favor of the latter place. In 1693 there had been already, certainly for eight years, a fort here, and there was near it at that time a Jesuit mission ; and doubtless here occurred the first conveyance of real estate in what is now Illinois executed within its boundaries, which this ancient document evidences. It is fitting and fortunate that it should, two hundred years after its execution, come into the possession of the Historical Society of Chicago to be preserved sacredly by it."

With the latter paragraph the present writer takes issue ; and those who have followed this narrative thus far will understand that however Mr. Mason's civic pride might claim the deed as executed on Chicago's soil, all the facts are against such a conclusion. Fort St. Louis was Acau's (or Ako's) home as well as La Forest's at that time ; it was the capital of the Illinois country and the centre of La Forest's and Tonty's operations; and though a fort was doubtless there on the lake shore, it was a mere station without importance or regular garrison or settlers. either whites or Indians,—a depot for the deposit of furs for shipment by lake to Canada.* The deed was in all probability signed at the fort at Starved Rock.

* See La Salle's reference to Chicago in certain of his reports. Translation in the *Magazine of American History*, Vol. I, p 553.

"MARQUETTE'S CROSS"

The most interesting of the relics of Starved Rock's ancient days is the remarkable cross, of which the above is a picture made from a recent photograph (full size of the original.) It was found near the Rock, and is the property of Col. D. F. Hitt. It is said to be one of the insignia of an archbishop. By some it has been called Marquette's Cross; but it is hardly probable that that modest hero ever owned it. He never held any rank as a churchman above that of priest; and notwithstanding the fact that the early missionaries frequently exercised the powers of the church's officials of much higher rank, and may even have worn their insignia, nevertheless the location in which it was found is against the probability of Marquette's connection with this particular cross. Marquette at most was at the Kaskaskia village near Starved Rock not to exceed fifteen days. During those days he was busy trying to save souls ; and seeing that the Indian village was on the north bank of the river and a mile west of the Rock, which was at that time wholly unoccupied, it is not likely that Marquette ever put his foot on that side of the river. The cross may have belonged to one of the priests named in the chapter on "The Missions."

In explaining, or in endeavoring to explain, the presence of this cross (which is not, as he says, pure gold, but rather brass covered originally with black enamel), Matson* says: "The Archbishop of Rouen sent to Canada one satin robe, and a large gold cross, with other emblems, to be given to the most devoted priest in America. The fathers awarded these gifts to Father Chrisp, chaplain of Fort St. Louis, but he died before their arrival, and in the fall of 1688 these things were presented to Father [Abbe] Cavelier, brother of La Salle. It is possible," concludes our author, "that the cross herewith may be the one referred to, and was lost by the owner during his rambles around the Rock."

This is all very interesting, but I am quite of the opinion that there is even less of pure gold in the story than in the cross ; and it certainly is a surprise to know that the Abbe Cavelier had ever been awarded a prize for his piety. No one now-a-days would have suspected it. However, this cross is not gold, as before remarked.

OTHER CURIOS.

Many minor relics have been found near the Rock, mostly articles of jewelry, coins of small value, medals, etc.; and Col. Hitt has unearthed also remains of French underground furnaces or bake-ovens near the Rock, and now wears a heavy gold ring found there.

Near Ottawa, some years ago, a small cannon was found, which consisted of a welded tube† of iron, about an inch and a half in calibre,

*MATSON: "*Pioneers of Illinois.*"
†PARKMAN : "*La Salle, etc.*"

strengthened by a series of thick iron rings, cooled on after the most ancient as well as the most modern methods of making cannon. It was fourteen inches long, the part near the muzzle having been burst off. Its construction was very rude, and it may have been made by a French blacksmith. As the work of a European cannon maker, it would have been antiquated even in the time of De Soto or Coronado.

The apparent pits in the soil on the top of the Rock may be the remains of holes dug by credulous traders early in the last century, who believed they might find gold buried there by Tonty; but as the "coin" of the Illinois in those days was "current beaver" rather than *Louis-d'or*, it is not recorded that any of the gold seekers found reward for their labor.

But the noblest of all the relics of Starved Rock is its history; and it stands as a monument to those weak ones of earth whose mortal sufferings here were, in God's mysterious wisdom, not the least of the many contributions of human sacrifice which have preserved to the people of the Illinois valley, and of the United States, and of the world, the priceless heritage of English Liberty.